That You May Know

Assurances from God in His Word

Terry Zuehsow

Scripture references marked ESV are personalized from the The Holy Bible, English Standard Version (ESV): Scripture quotations from the ESV® Bible (The Holy Bible, English Standard Version®), copyright © 2001 by Crossway, a publishing ministry of Good News Publishers. Used by permission. All rights reserved.

Scripture references marked KJV are personalized from the Authorized (King James) Version of the Bible (KJV): Scripture quotations from The Authorized (King James) Version. Rights in the Authorized Version in the United Kingdom are vested in the Crown. Reproduced by permission of the Crown's patentee, Cambridge University Press.

Scripture references marked NASB are personalized from the New American Standard Bible (NASB): Scripture quotations taken from the New American Standard Bible® (NASB). Copy-right © 1960, 1962, 1963, 1968, 1971, 1973, 1975, 1977, 1995 by the Lockman Foundation. Used by permission. www.Lockman.org

Scripture references marked NIV are personalized from the NEW INTERNATIONAL VER-SION (NIV): Scripture taken from the Holy Bible, NEW INTERNATIONAL VERSION®, NIV® Copyright © 1973, 1978, 1984, 2011 by Biblica, Inc.® Used by permission. All rights reserved worldwide.
Scripture references marked NKJV are personalized from the New King James Version (NKJV): Scripture taken from the New King James Version. Copyright © 1982 by Thomas Nelson, Inc. Used by permission. All rights reserved.

Scripture references marked NLT are personalized from the Holy Bible, New Living Translation (NLT): Scripture quotations marked NLT are taken from the Holy Bible, New Living Transla-tion, copyright © 1996, 2004, 2015 by Tyndale House Foundation. Used by permission of Tyndale House Publishers, Inc., Carol Stream, Illinois 60188. All rights reserved.

Scripture references marked RSV are personalized from the Revised Standard Version (RSV): Scripture quotations marked RSV are from Revised Standard Version of the Bible, copyright © 1946, 1952, and 1971 National Council of the Churches of Christ in the United States of Amer-ica. Used by permission. All rights reserved worldwide.

Cover photo by Dimitris Panagiotaras on Unsplash: unsplash.com/photos/xJWWp-Fpdjs.

Zuehsow, Terry W.
    That You May Know: Assurances from God in His Word by Terry W.Zuehsow
    ISBN 13: 978-1-943518-28-9
    Library of Congress Control Number:2019910877

Publication facilitated by McKinney Publishing
www.mckinneypublishing.com

Printed in the United States of America

Foreword

Dear Friends,

What a blessing it is to see this book in the works. The theme or purpose is to apply or personalize God's Word to our lives—our joys, our tough times and every situation.

We are promised in Isaiah 55:11[1] that God's Word will not return void:

> *So shall my word be that goeth forth out of my mouth: it shall not return unto me void, but it shall accomplish that which I please, and it shall prosper in the thing whereto I sent it.*

A neat feature of this book is that you can personalize it by writing in your name or have it printed in the book. A verse shared in the book, Isaiah 43:1[2], says:

> *I have called you by name, you are mine.*

My late husband, Dr. Frank Minirth, loved God's Word and loved sharing it with everyone in his life—family, friends, and patients. I remember him walking around with Scripture memory cards in his pocket and spending a lot of time in the Word. He wrote numerous books and workbooks addressing different life situations with God's Word and how it can be applied in each circumstance.

So how can a doctor mix or combine medicine and Scripture? My husband would offer clients all appropriate medical options plus a scriptural prescription if they were open to it. He often said, "Claim that verse." Psalm 119:11[1] says:

> *Thy word have I hid in mine heart.*

It is fit that the Word, being more precious than gold, yea than much fine gold, a peerless pearl: should not be laid up in the porter's lodge only—the outward ear; but even in the cabinet of the mind.[3]

Romans 12:2[1] says:

> *And be not conformed to this world: but be ye transformed by the renewing of your mind, that ye may prove what is that good, and acceptable, and perfect, will of God.*

These verses say that we can read, memorize, apply and make Scripture a part of our lives, mind, and heart.

In recent years I did a lot of life coaching. My favorite and most pertinent verse I often shared was 2 Timothy 1:7[1]:

> *For God hath not given us a spirit of fear; but of power, and of love, and a sound mind.*

Take a moment and put your name in this verse.

Please read, enjoy, and take to heart these wonderful messages from God's Word.

In Christ,
Mary Alice Minirth

---

[1] KJV
[2] ESV
[3] From Commentary/Precept Austin by Dean Boys, quoted by James Ford, William Cowper

Acknowledgements

What an amazing journey this has been! I joyfully acknowledge my daughter Sara, who, in the midst of deep pain from a shattered relationship and an unexpected journey into single parenthood, desired a personalized collection of God's promises (and didn't know that I was working on one). She and my other daughter, Kate, have been invaluable in helping me edit and market this devotional book.

I am indebted to Joshua Hansard, a brother in Christ that was also healing from a similarly devastating situation. He introduced me to several books about God's ongoing activity in our lives, through which I was inspired to envision this book in its current form. I am thankful for my pastor, David Thompson, who has encouraged me throughout this endeavor, diligently reviewing my work and helping me resolve critical theological issues.

I am thankful for my team of editors, including Kristen E. Clark, Kim Parker Nyman, Rick Nyman, and Michael J. Sweeney. I especially appreciate my beloved wife, Angi, who has been very supportive and has graciously allowed me the time necessary to bring this concept to fruition over many months. She has lovingly assisted me in a careful review of the text and in ensuring the accuracy of the selected Bible verses.

Above all, I humbly and gratefully acknowledge the Triune God— Father, Son, and Holy Spirit—who has given us His amazing and excellent promises and assurances. I begin to see how the specific gifts, abilities, and experiences that the Lord has provided me over the years have made such a book possible, and I recognize that He has guided and enabled me throughout the book's development. God in Christ has demonstrated yet again His power and commitment to work all things together for good for those that love Him and are called according to His purpose.

To God be the glory!

TABLE OF CONTENTS

Always with the Lord

All Things Made New

YOUR TRIP SUMMARY

That You May Know

YOUR ITINERARY

Welcome to the start of a unique journey into all God has done, is doing, and will do for you. Although the assurances of God presented in the following chapters apply to all believers in Jesus Christ, it is my prayer that you will personalize each promise in your own heart and mind.

Every good thing that is in you

The Apostle Paul sent a brief letter to his friend Philemon. In it Paul prayed that Philemon and all those he engages might gain a "full knowledge of every good thing that is in us for the sake of Christ."[1] So what all is included in "every good thing"? Have you ever meditated about all that is now yours as a believer in the Lord Jesus Christ? Have you wondered about God's thoughts concerning you from before the universe began? Have you considered what all changed for you when Jesus Christ died on the cross, arose from the dead, and ascended into heaven on your behalf? How much do you know about God's promises for you day-to-day, moment-by-moment during your life here on earth? And what can you confidently look forward to after this life is over?

Several years ago, one of my Bible teachers was considering John 3:16 with us:

> For God so loved the world that He gave His only Son, that whoever believes in Him should not perish but have eternal life. (RSV)

In order to deepen our individual connection with this familiar Bible verse, the teacher suggested that we insert our own names in place of the more general nouns and pronouns. Try that with your name in the blanks:

> For God so loved you, _____, that He gave His only Son for you. You believe in Him, and you will not perish, _____, but have eternal life.

That felt remarkably different to me. How did you react?

I was able to identify over 1600 promises and assurances throughout the Bible. After selecting a Bible translation for each, I personalized them by referring to the reader as "you." Then I integrated them all by topic into 230 conversational paragraphs, taking great care to

---

[1] Philemon 1:6 ESV

preserve the original wording and intent.[2] Through this endeavor, by
God's grace I am now seeing Scripture through new lenses—not lead-
ing to any new doctrines, but definitely to deeper love and excitement!
It is my distinct joy to share those lenses with you.

Reading past God's promises
At times I have tended to gloss over the promises in God's Word, and
to focus instead on what *I* should be doing—trying to keep God's Law.
I mistakenly assumed that, since God already did so much for me, it
was now primarily up to me to do my best for Him. Whenever I suc-
cumb to such thinking, I become less peaceful, more driven, and less
loving. I feel the weight of living a "Christian life" squarely on my
own shoulders. This typically leaves me feeling either self-right-
eously proud or woefully inadequate.

Paul very much wanted to help us avoid this trap. He dedicated the
entire first half of his letter to the Ephesians exclusively to remarkable
facts about:
1. YESTERDAY: what God has already accomplished for you,
2. TODAY: what God is doing today in your life, and
3. FOREVER: what God will continue to do for you into eternity.

Paul earnestly prayed that you would realize this and take it fully to
heart:

> *For this reason, because I have heard of your faith in the
> Lord Jesus and your love toward all the saints, I do not cease
> to give thanks for you, remembering you in my prayers, that
> the God of our Lord Jesus Christ, the Father of glory, may
> give you the Spirit of wisdom and of revelation in the
> knowledge of Him, having the eyes of your hearts enlight-
> ened, **that you may know** what is the hope to which He has
> called you (YESTERDAY), what are the riches of His glori-
> ous inheritance in the saints (FOREVER), and what is the
> immeasurable greatness of His power toward us who believe
> (TODAY), according to the working of His great might that*

---

[2] All passages in subsequent chapters
are personalized from translations
of the Bible, including ESV,
NASB, NIV, NKJV, NLT and
RSV. Pronouns referring to Deity
are capitalized for respect and refer-
ential clarity. Source passages and
selected Bible versions are simply
listed in the footnotes. See p.155
for Bible book abbreviations. See
website thatyoumayknowbook.com
to order personalized copies with
reader's name interspersed.

He worked in Christ when He raised Him from the dead and seated Him at His right hand in the heavenly places, far above all rule and authority and power and dominion, and above every name that is named, not only in this age but also in the one to come. [3]

Feeling unlovable

I suspect we all struggle at times feeling like God's assurances don't fully apply to us. Sometimes you may feel alone, afraid, unloved, unlovable, abandoned, or hopeless. You may accept that God *has* to love you because of what Christ did, but you are not always sure that He *likes* you very much. Perhaps you see yourself as a second-class Christian, of limited value, usefulness, and significance to God. On occasion you might even feel like a failure or an embarrassment to Him.

If you experience such feelings, you are actually in good company. Try doing a quick survey of the first few verses of each Psalm. In a quarter of them you will discover many similar feelings and fears expressed passionately. But you will also find in these same Psalms confessions of the reality and certainty of God's assurances and the hope and comfort that they bring—honest feelings, met by powerful and rock-solid promises.

How God really feels about you

How does God actually feel about you? He loves you passionately and forever! [4] We learn from the Scriptures that even before Creation began, God was thinking about you and chose you to be His own. [5] And He never changes! [6]

But why would God populate His perfect universe with people like us, who were free to reject Him? If God knew full well that the people He created would spurn His love, fall into sin, and fundamentally damage His creation, why even go through with it at all? Why didn't He just make us so we *had* to love Him? Think about it. If you *had* to love your parents, spouse, child, or friend, would that really be love?

God's everlasting love for you

Apparently it was and is so important to God that you genuinely love Him, that He was willing to endure all the sin, evil, and even death on

---

[3] Eph 1:15-21 ESV, with annotations
[4] Jer 31:3

[5] Eph 1:3-6
[6] Mal 3:6; Jas 1:17; Heb 13:8

a cross in order that He might finally achieve an eternal love relationship with you.[7] From the very beginning, Jesus's death and resurrection were part of God's plan to make you holy and to woo you to Himself.[8] Jesus declared that God's greatest desire is that you "love the Lord your God with all your heart and with all your soul and with all your strength and with all your mind."[9]

The Apostle John reminds us that our love for God is only made possible by Him having first loved us.[10] Jesus wants you to know that both He and His Father love you as much as They love each other![11] Imagine how great that love must be! God treasures you,[12] you are precious to Him,[13] and you are His delight.[14] He rejoices over you and is glad in you.[15] Every little detail about you is precious to Him, from when you were first knit together in your mother's womb[16] to the day you die to be with Him.[17] He has numbered the hairs on your head.[18] Apparently He even journals about you![19]

A tool for believers in Christ
That You May Know is not intended to replace your Bible reading, but to serve as a supporting devotional tool. This book does not chronicle God's involvement in history, which reveals much about God's character and confirms the certainty of prophecies yet to be fulfilled. It speaks little about living in a God-pleasing manner, although being grounded in God's assurances makes possible the life of good works that our Lord prepared for you to walk in.[20] Nor does this book substantially address God's wrath and judgment, hell, or the influence of the devil, the world, and your own sinful flesh, although it is only through God's mighty promises that you experience His grace and are empowered to confess your sins, receive God's forgiveness, and ultimately be victorious over evil.

True Christian faith is grounded in the cross of Jesus Christ[21]—on your dependence upon God for forgiveness and restoration.[22] Focusing exclusively on God's assurances apart from the full context of His Word might delude some into expecting heaven on earth—a life free today

---

[7] Heb 12:1-2
[8] 1Pet 1:18-21; Acts 2:23-24
[9] Luke 10:27 ESV
[10] 1John 4:19 ESV
[11] John 15:9; 17:23
[12] Ex 19:5 NIV
[13] Is 43:4
[14] Is 62:4 NASB
[15] Is 65:19 NASB
[16] Ps 139:13 NIV
[17] Ps 116:15
[18] Luke 12:7
[19] Ps 56:8 NASB
[20] Eph 2:10 NASB
[21] Gal 6:14
[22] 1John 1:8-9

from temptation, sin, disappointment, sorrow, troubles, and persecution. That day is indeed coming when, either through death or the Lord's return, you will experience such perfection for eternity. Today, however, your Lord reminds you, "In the world you will have tribulation. But take heart; I have overcome the world."[23] Even in this fallen world, "we know that for those who love God all things work together for good, for those who are called according to His purpose."[24] In the midst of it all, "we are more than conquerors through Him who loved us."[25] Christ's parting words to us before ascending into heaven were "…surely I am with you always, to the very end of the age."[26]

Intended audience
As you've probably surmised, this collection of personalized promises is specifically targeted to Christians, who believe in the one true God—Father, Son (Jesus Christ), and Holy Spirit.[27] By the power of this Holy Spirit believers acknowledge and confess their sins and trust in Jesus Christ's atoning sacrifice for them on the cross. The Spirit enables them to grow in their love for God and for all who belong to Him.[28] And they are assured of spending eternity together with God and all believers in His glorious Kingdom.[29]

Assuming this describes you, an exciting journey through the multi-faceted assurances of God awaits you. If you happen to be reading this book but are not a believer at this time, I pray that what follows will help paint for you a compelling picture of all that God in Christ has done for you and of His unchanging will to be in a loving relationship with you both today and forever.

What God says about His promises
The Apostle Peter wrote that God's divine power has granted to you all things that pertain to life and godliness, through the knowledge of Him who called you to His own glory and excellence, by which He has granted to you His precious and very great promises.[30] These

---

[23] John 16:33 ESV
[24] Rom 8:28 ESV
[25] Rom 8:37 NKJV
[26] Matt 28:20 NIV
[27] Matt 28:19. The Bible uses multiple names, titles, and descriptors for the one true God ("I Am"— rendered "LORD" in the Old Testament, the Almighty, the Blessed, the Most High, the Ancient of Days) and for the three persons of the Trinity: the Father (heavenly Father, Abba); the Son of God (Jesus, Messiah/Christ, Son of Man, Lord, Savior, Redeemer, Good Shepherd, Lamb of God); and the Holy Spirit (Spirit, Spirit of God, Comforter, Counselor).
[28] Gal 5:22-23
[29] Rev 21:3
[30] 2Pet 1:3-4 ESV

marvelous promises serve as a sure and steadfast anchor for your soul.[31] Our Lord, who made these promises to you, is faithful,[32] and you can be certain that all God's promises find their Yes in Jesus Christ,[33] His beloved Son.

Praying for you
May God richly bless your journey through this book, and may you fall in love with Him more and more. Before reading each topic, I suggest inviting the Holy Spirit to open your heart and mind so that God's Word may have its full effect on you. Please do not rush through it—take your time and meditate on all that is now yours in Christ. It is always appropriate to ask the question, "Where did God say *that*?" Examine the verse references whenever you wish and use them to further explore the sections of Scripture from which individual assurances have been drawn. And you are certainly encouraged to revisit this book as God leads you. Above all, please *do* take it personally!

I invite you to savor Paul's prayer for you found in Ephesians chapter three:

> *For this reason I bow my knees before the Father, from whom every family in heaven and on earth is named, that according to the riches of His glory He may grant you to be strengthened with power through His Spirit in your inner being, so that Christ may dwell in your heart through faith—that you, being rooted and grounded in love, may have strength to comprehend with all the saints what is the breadth and length and height and depth, and to know the love of Christ that surpasses knowledge, that you may be filled with all the fullness of God. Now to Him who is able to do far more abundantly than all that you ask or think, according to the power at work within you, to Him be glory in the church and in Christ Jesus throughout all generations, forever and ever. Amen.[34]*

---

[31] Heb 6:19 ESV
[32] Heb 10:23; Ps 145:13 ESV

[33] 2Cor 1:20 ESV
[34] Eph 3:14-21 ESV, personalized

Your Itinerary

7

That You May Know

YESTERDAY
You know what is the hope to which God has called you.[1]

"It is finished!"[2] That was Jesus's proclamation to you from the cross. What was finished? That's the focus of this section. Here you can reflect on all that God has already accomplished in and for you through His Son's life, death, and resurrection. Here you are reminded of God's love for you from eternity and of everything that is now true for you in Christ.

This section doesn't deal with things that are happening today or that may happen someday. It's not about what you must do or about levels of holiness you must achieve. It is exclusively about what God Himself has done to break the power and consequences of sin within you. In Christ, everything that stood in the way of your perfect love relationship with God has been fully dealt with.

If you ever find yourself wondering whether you are good enough to get into heaven, ask yourself what part of Jesus Christ's sacrifice for you was insufficient or inadequate. Since it was complete, just as He declared, you are on very solid ground indeed! You are free to live in complete confidence that all of God's *yesterday* assurances are absolutely true for you, now and always.

---

[1] Eph 1:18 ESV   [2] John 19:30 ESV

Yesterday

__Those God Foreknew He Also Predestined__[1]

Do you realize that you have been on God's mind and in His heart from before creation? Your presence at this time in history and in this place is not by accident or chance, but by God's deliberate design. In Christ He has provided you all that you need to live securely, meaningfully, and effectively.

1. Beloved Before Time Began

> How amazing that God loved you even before the beginning of time! Scripture showcases the ultimate love story, exploring God's timeless, costly, and unchanging love for you. He created the universe and, even before that, He planned the sacrifice of His Son, all for you. He intended for you to have a true love relationship with Him, and it couldn't have been real love if you were not given the ability and freedom to reject Him. He has always loved you, and He has enabled you to love Him.

Everlasting love: You have come to know and believe the everlasting love that God has for you.[2] Our Lord Jesus Christ Himself and God our Father love you.[3] The Lord God of heaven, the great, mighty, and awesome God, established and keeps His everlasting covenant of love with you.[4] God, who is rich in mercy, greatly loves you.[5]

Redeeming love: God loved you and gave His one and only Son as an atoning sacrifice for your sins.[6] With the Lord there is steadfast love[7] and plentiful redemption.[8] The Lord God is slow to anger toward you,[9] and His soul shall not abhor you.[10] The Lord loves you freely, for His anger has turned from you.[11]

---

[1] Rom 8:29 NIV
[2] 1John 4:16; Jer 31:3 NASB
[3] 2Thes 2:13,16 NKJV; *cf.* Deut 7:8,13; 33:3; 2Chron 9:8; Is 43:4; Gal 2:20;

1Thes 1:4; Jude 1:21; Rev 1:5
[4] Neh 1:5; 9:32; Ezek 16:60,62 NIV; *cf.* 1King 8:23; 2Chron 6:14
[5] Eph 2:4 NIV
[6] 1John 4:10-11; John 3:16 NIV

[7] Ps 130:7 ESV
[8] Ps 130:7; 1Cor 1:30 ESV
[9] Ex 34:6 NIV; *cf.* Jonah 4:2
[10] Lev 26:11 ESV
[11] Hos 14:4 NIV

10

Steadfast love: Truly the Lord God is good to you.[12] He delights in showing steadfast love for you.[13] The Lord is a gracious God, merciful to you and abounding in steadfast love.[14] For as high as the heavens are above the earth, so great is the Lord's steadfast love toward you.[15] His steadfast love and faithfulness to you endure forever and will ever preserve you.[16] The steadfast love of the Lord to you never ceases[17] and shall not depart from you,[18] as it is from everlasting to everlasting.[19]

..." I have loved you with an everlasting love..."

Jeremiah 31:3 NASB

---

[12] Ps 73:1; 100:5 ESV;
cf. 1Chron 16:34;
2Chron 5:13; 7:3;
Ezra 3:11; Tit 3:4
[13] Micah 7:18;
Deut 5:10 ESV;
cf. 1King 8:23;
2Chron 6:14;
Neh 1:5; 9:32
[14] Jonah 4:2 ESV
[15] Ps 103:11 ESV;
cf. Ps 117:2
[16] 1Chron 16:34;
Ps 40:11 ESV;
cf. Deut 7:9;
2Chron 5:13; 7:3;
Ezra 3:11;
Ps 100:5; 117:2
[17] Lam 3:22 ESV
[18] Is 54:10 ESV
[19] Ps 103:17 ESV

2. Highly Valued

When my parents told others something they appreciated about me, I recall feeling very special and loved. But proud parents that show pictures and share stories about their children have nothing on God! God highly values you, and He describes you in His Word as His treasured possession, His crown of beauty, His delight, and His source of joy. Perhaps you're asking, "Me? Really?" Absolutely!

His heart: You are precious in the Lord's sight.[1] The Lord sets His heart on you.[2] You are the apple of the His eye.[3] The Lord blesses you;[4] God is for you.[5] You are included in the Lord's book of remembrance of those who fear Him and esteem His name.[6]

His treasure: The Lord makes so much of you[7] and has zeal for you.[8] You are honored by the Lord[9] and are holy to Him.[10] The Lord of hosts declares that you are His treasured possession.[11] You are a crown of beauty in the hand of the Lord, and a royal diadem in the hand of your God.[12]

His delight: God is pleased with you.[13] You shall be called My Delight Is in You; for the Lord delights in you.[14] The Lord brought you out into a broad place; He rescued you because He delights in you.[15]

His joy: The Lord God rejoices over you with gladness[16] and with singing.[17] The Lord makes His face shine on you[18] and lifts up his countenance on you.[19] As the bridegroom rejoices over the bride, so God rejoices over you.[20]

---

[1] Is 43:4 NKJV
[2] Job 7:17 ESV
[3] Deut 32:10 NKJV
[4] Deut 7:13 NKJV
[5] Ps 56:9 NASB
[6] Mal 3:16 NASB
[7] Job 7:17 ESV
[8] Is 26:11 NASB
[9] Is 43:4 NKJV

[10] Deut 7:6 NKJV;
cf. Deut 26:19
[11] Ex 19:5;
Mal 3:17 ESV;
cf. Deut 7:6;
26:18
[12] Is 62:3 NASB
[13] Luke 2:14 NASB
[14] Is 62:4 NASB

[15] 2Sam 22:20 NASB
[16] Zeph 3:17 ESV;
cf. Is 65:19
[17] Zeph 3:17 NKJV
[18] Num 6:25 NASB
[19] Num 6:26 NASB
[20] Is 62:5 NASB

...And as the bridegroom
rejoices over the bride,
So your God will rejoice over you.
Isaiah 62:5 NASB

3. All in God's Plan

What a precious comfort and assurance to know that God elected you in Christ before creation to be His very own! You may wonder how that fits with your ability to freely love God, or the fact that not everyone goes to heaven. Paul shares two things to help you with this: God's reasoning is way beyond yours,[1] and God is never unjust.[2] Apparently God decided that the good news of His choosing you was much too exciting and important to keep secret!

Known in advance: God foreknew you.[3] You are among the elect of God the Father,[4] according to His foreknowledge.[5] In the Lord's book were written all the days fashioned for you when as yet there were none of them.[6]

Predestined to belong: God predestined you to be conformed to the image of His Son.[7] In love God predestined you for adoption to Himself as His child through Jesus Christ.[8]

And destined for salvation: God has destined you to obtain salvation through our Lord Jesus Christ.[9] God saved you because of His own purpose and grace, which he gave you in Christ Jesus before the ages began.[10] Your name has been written before the foundation of the world in the book of life of the Lamb who was slain.[11]

---

[1] Rom 11:33
[2] Rom 9:14
[3] Rom 8:29 NIV
[4] Tit 1:1;
 1Pet 1:2 NKJV
[5] 1Pet 1:2 NKJV
[6] Ps 139:16 NKJV
[7] Rom 8:29 NIV
[8] Eph 1:4-5 ESV
[9] 1Thes 5:9 ESV
[10] 2Tim 1:9 ESV
[11] Rev 13:8 ESV;
 cf. Rev 20:15

[God] saved us and called us to a holy calling, not because of our works but because of His own purpose and grace, which He gave us in Christ Jesus before the ages began.

2 Timothy 1:9 ESV

And Those He Predestined, He Also Called[1]

Vocation is a Bible word that has become part of our everyday language. Literally it means one's "calling" in life. Who do you suppose is doing the calling? And exactly what has He called you to? You are invited to dive into God's Word and explore!

4. Called by Name

How do you feel when a person you've met only briefly in the past remembers your name and details about your life—important and respected? God Himself has called you by name with a call that can never be taken back. He has graciously and earnestly reached out to you. He has called you with the sure hope of salvation into a new and vibrant life in His kingdom. Yes, He most assuredly knows your name!

Personally: The Lord God has called you[2] by name.[3] He called you to a holy calling, which was granted you in Christ Jesus from all eternity.[4] Jesus came to call you,[5] and you know the hope to which God has called you.[6]

Proactively: You are called "Sought After."[7] The Lord God has visited you.[8] The Son of Man came to seek and to save you.[9] God called you through the Gospel:[10] Christ suffered once for sins to bring you to God.[11]

Purposefully: You were called by God according to His own purpose[12] and grace.[13] The Lord God has called you in righteousness[14] and holiness.[15] You have been called to be a saint.[16] God calls you into His

---

[1] Rom 8:30 NIV
[2] Is 43:1 NKJV; *cf.* Is 42:6; Joel 2:32; Rom 8:28; 1Cor 1:24; Eph 1:18; 1Thes 2:12; 2Thes 2:14; 2Tim 1:9; Rev 17:14

[3] Is 43:1 NASB
[4] 2Tim 1:9 NASB
[5] Matt 9:13 NIV
[6] Eph 1:18 NIV
[7] Is 62:12 NIV
[8] Luke 1:68 NASB
[9] Luke 19:10 NASB
[10] 2Thes 2:14 NASB

[11] 1Pet 3:18 NIV
[12] Rom 8:28; 2Tim 1:9 NKJV
[13] 2Tim 1:9 NKJV
[14] Is 42:6 NKJV
[15] 1Thes 4:7 NKJV
[16] 1Cor 1:2 NKJV

own kingdom and glory.[17] You share in the heavenly calling with all believers.[18]

"... I have called you by name; you are Mine!"
Isaiah 43:1 NASB

---

[17] 1Thes 2:12 NKJV   [18] Heb 3:1 NIV

5. Chosen Before the Foundation of the World

Have you ever attended a renewal of wedding vows? One spouse might look into the other's eyes and say, "If I had it all to do over, I would still choose you!" How would you feel if those words were directed to you—honored? special? loved? Even though God is fully aware of your faults and shortcomings, He renews His vows to you daily! You did not choose Him, but He has freely chosen you to be His own. He has chosen you to grow in grace, in faith, and in love. Are you feeling special yet?

Chosen for Himself: The Lord set His love on you.[1] He chose you[2] to be His own, His treasured possession,[3] and brings you near to Him.[4] The Lord has set you apart for Himself,[5] a person for His Name.[6] God chose you in Christ before the foundation of the world that you should be holy and blameless before Him.[7] You are part of His chosen people, a holy nation.[8]

Given a heritage: God has given you the heritage of those who fear His name.[9] Your steps are established by the Lord.[10] Through Jesus Christ you have gained access by faith into the grace in which you now stand.[11] The abundant grace of God through Jesus Christ reigns and abounds in your life.[12] God from the beginning chose you for salvation through sanctification by the Spirit and belief in the truth,[13] and to be rich in faith.[14] Christ Jesus came into the world to save sinners, including you.[15] It was God's desire that you be saved and come to the knowledge of the truth.[16]

[1] Deut 7:7 NASB
[2] John 15:16 NASB; cf. Deut 7:6-7; 10:15; Ps 65:4; 105:6; 135:4; Is 41:9; 44:1; Zech 2:12; Mark 13:20; Col 3:12; 1Thes 1:4; Jas 2:5;
Rev 17:14
[3] Ps 135:4 NIV
[4] Ps 65:4 NASB
[5] Ps 4:3 NASB; cf. Lev 20:26
[6] Acts 15:14 NASB
[7] Eph 1:4 NASB
[8] 1Pet 2:9 NIV
[9] Ps 61:5 NIV
[10] Ps 37:23 NASB
[11] Rom 5:2 NIV
[12] Rom 5:15,17 ESV
[13] 2Thes 2:13 NKJV
[14] Jas 2:5 NKJV
[15] 1Tim 1:15 NKJV
[16] 1Tim 2:4 NKJV

...[God] chose us in [Christ]
before the foundation of the
world, that we would be holy
and blameless before Him....
Ephesian 1:4 NASB

6. Fearfully and Wonderfully Made

You know that God created the universe and everything in it, but perhaps sometimes you might forget that He specially designed and formed *you*—cell-by-cell, with your unique DNA, mind, heart, and soul. He made you *exactly* as He intended. You are His masterpiece. Though blurred by sin, you still bear the image of your Father in heaven. You are rational, creative, and purposeful. He has high hopes and big plans for you, all leading to His glory and to your perfect joy.

Created by God: The Lord, the one God, created[1] and formed you.[2] You have been fearfully and wonderfully[3] made.[4] You are the clay, and the Lord is your potter.[5] His hands made and fashioned you,[6] forming your inward parts and knitting you together in your mother's womb.[7] There the Lord's eyes saw your unformed substance.[8] The Lord also made your soul[9] and formed your spirit within you.[10] He made you through His Spirit, and the breath of the Almighty gives you life.[11] Your life and breath are in the hand of the God of heaven.[12] God has determined your number of months and days.[13] In Him you live and move and have your being.[14] God made everything, including you, for its own purpose.[15]

Made in His image: God made you[16] in His own image,[17] after His likeness.[18] You are from God[19] and have been born of Him.[20] God's seed abides in you.[21] He established you[22] to rule over the fish in the sea and the birds in the sky and over every living creature that moves

---

[1] Mal 2:10; Is 43:1,7; Deut 32:6 ESV

[2] Is 44:21 NKJV; cf. Is 43:1; 44:24; Ps 139:13

[3] Ps 139:14 NKJV

[4] Ps 139:14 NKJV; cf. Deut 32:6; Job 35:10; Ps 100:3

[5] Is 64:8 NKJV

[6] Ps 119:73 NKJV; cf. Ps 138:8; Is 64:8

[7] Ps 139:13 ESV; cf. Is 44:2,24

[8] Ps 139:16 NASB

[9] Jer 38:16 NKJV

[10] Zech 12:1 NKJV

[11] Job 33:4 NKJV

[12] Job 12:10 NKJV; cf. Dan 5:23

[13] Job 14:5 NKJV

[14] Acts 17:28 NKJV

[15] Prov 16:4 NASB

[16] Deut 32:6 NASB; cf. Is 43:7; 44:2; 54:5

[17] Gen 1:26-27 NASB; cf. Gen 9:6

[18] Gen 1:26 ESV

[19] 1John 4:4 ESV; cf. 1John 5:19

[20] John 1:13 NASB; cf. 1John 3:9; 4:7; 5:1,4

[21] 1John 3:9 NASB

[22] Deut 32:6 NASB

on the ground.[23] You exist for God and through Jesus Christ.[24] The Lord created you for His glory.[25]

I will praise You, for I am fearfully and wonderfully made; Marvelous are your works, And that my soul knows very well.

Psalm 139:14 NKJV

---

[23] Gen 1:26,28 NIV   [24] 1Cor 8:6 NASB   [25] Is 43:7 NASB

7. Made One Spirit with God

God reveals in His Word that there is more to you than your physical body or even just your body and mind. Part of you continues on in spite of physical death and bodily decay. You have a spirit, which, as a believer, is actively aligned and joined with God's Holy Spirit. What does it mean that God—Father, Son, and Holy Spirit—has taken up residence in you? May you continue to find out day by day.

The Father in you: God lives in you[1] and has made His home with you.[2] He has given to you His exceedingly great and precious promises, that through these you have become a partaker of the divine nature.[3]

Christ in you: The glory Jesus' Father gave to Jesus, Jesus gives to you.[4] You are joined to the Lord and have become one spirit with Him.[5] Christ is in you,[6] He has made His home with you,[7] and you share in Him.[8] You are found in Christ,[9] who was chosen before the creation of the world, but was revealed in these last times for your sake.[10] You have been crucified with Christ; and it is no longer you who live, but Christ lives in you.[11] For in Christ the whole fullness of deity dwells bodily, and you have been filled in Him, who is the head of all rule and authority.[12]

Filled with the Holy Spirit: You were made to drink of one Spirit.[13] The Lord God, the heavenly Father, has poured out His Spirit on you[14] richly[15] and put His Spirit within you[16] through Jesus Christ your Savior.[17] You have been baptized with the Holy Spirit[18] and fire.[19] You have received not the spirit of the world[20] but the Spirit who is from God.[21] You have been anointed by the Holy One, and that anointing

---

[1] 1John 4:15 NIV
[2] John 14:23 NKJV
[3] 2Pet 1:4 NKJV
[4] John 17:22 NKJV
[5] 1Cor 6:17 ESV
[6] John 14:20;
   Rom 8:10;
   Col 1:27 NKJV
[7] John 14:23 NKJV
[8] Heb 3:14 NIV
[9] Phil 3:9 NIV
[10] 1Pet 1:20 NIV
[11] Gal 2:20 NASB
[12] Col 2:9-10 ESV
[13] 1Cor 12:13 NASB
[14] Joel 2:28-29;
   Acts 2:17-18;
   Ezek 39:29 NKJV;
   cf. Titus 3:6
[15] Tit 3:6 NASB
[16] Ezek 36:27 NASB;
   cf. Luke 11:13;
   Acts 5:32;
   1John 4:4,13
[17] Tit 3:6 NASB
[18] Matt 3:11; Mark
   1:8; Luke 3:16;
   Acts 11:16 NASB
[19] Matt 3:11 NASB;
   cf. Luke 3:16
[20] 1Cor 2:12 NASB
[21] 1Cor 2:12 NASB;
   cf. Gal 3:2

abides in you.[22] The Spirit of glory and of God rests upon you.[23] God's temple is holy[24] and, together with all believers, you are that temple.[25] Your body is a temple of the Holy Spirit,[26] who dwells in you[27] forever.[28]

But whoever is united with the Lord is one with Him in spirit.
1 Corinthians 6:17 NIV

[22] 1John 2:20,27 ESV
[23] 1Pet 4:14 NASB
[24] 1Cor 3:17 ESV

[25] 1Cor 3:16-17 NIV
[26] 1Cor 6:19 NASB

[27] 2Tim 1:14 NASB; *cf.* Rom 8:9; 1Cor 3:16; 6:19
[28] John 14:16 NASB

8. Given the Gift of Faith

Exactly what is *faith*—agreement with a set of propositions or doctrines? That is certainly part of faith, but real faith runs much deeper than that. When my first daughter was very young, I took her up with me to see our attic. As I walked down the attic stairs ahead of her, they broke and I landed safely on the floor below. But my daughter, now alone in the attic, looked anxiously to me for help. I held out my arms and said, "Jump, I'll catch you!" Without hesitation she popped right out of the attic and into my arms. I realized that I had just witnessed a powerful example of genuine faith. She trusted me implicitly that I wouldn't let her fall. That is the kind of faith God produces in you by the mighty working of the Holy Spirit through His Word.

Brought to faith: Through Jesus Christ, the founder and perfecter of your faith,[1] you are a believer in God[2] and know Him[3] who is true.[4] God chose you to be rich in faith,[5] and the God of all grace Himself confirms you.[6] You have seen a great light; on you a light has shined.[7] You are receiving the end result of your faith, the salvation of your soul.[8]

Fully assured: You have full assurance of faith.[9] You believe that Jesus is the Son of God,[10] and you believe in His name.[11] The Lord gave you a heart[12] to know that Jesus Christ is your Lord,[13] and you know Him.[14] In Him you have boldness and confident access to God.[15] You have confidence to enter the Most Holy Place by the blood of Jesus.[16] You have obtained a faith of equal standing with Peter and the Apostles by the righteousness of your God and Savior Jesus Christ.[17]

Never abandoned: The Lord directs your heart into the love of God and into the steadfastness of Christ.[18] Jesus Christ will confess your

[1] Heb 12:2 ESV
[2] 1Pet 1:21 NASB
[3] 1John 4:7 NASB
[4] 1John 5:20 NASB
[5] Jas 2:5 NASB
[6] 1Pet 5:10 NASB
[7] Is 9:2 NKJV
[8] 1Pet 1:9 NIV
[9] Heb 10:22 NASB
[10] 1John 5:5 NASB
[11] 1John 5:13 NASB
[12] Jer 24:7 NASB
[13] Acts 10:36 NASB; cf. Jer 24:7; Ezek 20:44
[14] Phil 3:10 NASB
[15] Eph 3:12 NASB
[16] Heb 10:19 NIV
[17] 2Pet 1:1 ESV
[18] 2Thes 3:5 NASB

name before His Father and before His angels.[19] You will not be forgotten by the Lord,[20] who has engraved you on the palms of His hands.[21] The Lord God has not forsaken you[22] and will never leave you.[23] You are part of "A City Not Forsaken."[24] You look to the Lord and are radiant, and your face shall never be ashamed.[25]

...looking to Jesus, the founder and perfecter of our faith...

Hebrews 12:2 ESV

---

[19] Rev 3:5 NKJV;
  cf. Luke 12:8
[20] Is 44:21 NKJV
[21] Is 49:16 NIV

[22] Ps 9:10 NKJV;
  cf. Deut 4:31;
  Heb 13:5

[23] Heb 13:5 ESV;
  cf. Deut 4:31
[24] Is 62:12 NKJV
[25] Ps 34:5 NASB

9. Made Christ's Own

The ultimate put-down might well be, "You don't belong here." Few phrases have such power to deeply wound you to the core. Comedian Groucho Marx once quipped that he would never join a club that would accept him as a member. Do you ever feel that way about your membership in Jesus' church? How could a holy God ever include *you* in His club? The amazing fact is that God created the universe and planned the sacrifice of His Son just so that you could belong as an honored member in good standing. You have been baptized into Christ Jesus, into His death and His resurrection, and now everything that is His has become yours! May you thoroughly enjoy your lifetime (and beyond) membership!

Belongs: The Lord welcomes you.[1] You have been called by His Name.[2] You belong to God the Father[3] and to Jesus Christ, His Son.[4] The Lord took you[5] to be one of His people[6] for His own possession[7] forever.[8] You know[9] that the Lord is your God;[10] there is no other.[11] God is not ashamed to be called your God.[12] You are not your own,[13]

[1] 2Cor 6:17 NASB
[2] Acts 15:17 NASB
[3] Is 43:1 NIV; *cf.* 1Chron 29:11; Ps 24:1; Is 44:5; Mal 3:17; 2Tim 2:19
[4] 1Cor 15:23 NIV; *cf.* Rom 1:6; 1Cor 3:23; 2Cor 10:7
[5] Ex 6:7 ESV
[6] Rom 9:25 NKJV; *cf.* Ex 6:7; Lev 26:12; Deut 27:9; 32:9; 1Sam 12:22; 2King 9:6; 1Chron 17:21-22; Ps 79:13; 81:8; Is 63:8; Jer 30:22; 31:33; 32:28; Ezek 11:20; 34:30; 36:28; 37:23; Hos 2:1,23; Zech 2:11; 13:9; 2Cor 6:16; Heb 8:10; 1Pet 2:10
[7] 1Pet 2:9 NASB
[8] 1Chron 17:22 NASB
[9] Ex 6:7 NASB; *cf.* Ex 29:46; Ezek 20:20; 28:26; 34:30; Joel 2:27; Heb 8:11
[10] Jer 31:33 NASB; *cf.* Gen 17:7-8; Ex 6:7; 15:2; 29:45-46; Lev 11:44-45; 18:2,4,30; 19:2-4,10,25,31-33,36; 20:7,24; 23:22,28,40,43; 24:22; 25:17,38,55; 26:1,13; Num 15:41; Deut 4:31; 5:6; 8:5; 10:21; 20:4; 27:9; 30:6,9,20; 31:6; Josh 1:9; 1King 8:23; 2King 10:31; 18:5; 19:4,15,20; 21:12; 23:21; 1Chron 16:14; 17:24; 29:3; 2Chron 6:14; 9:8; Ezra 6:21-22; 7:6; 9:8,10,15; Neh 13:22; Ps 63:1; 86:2; Is 25:1,9; 41:10,13,17; Jer 30:22; 32:38; Ezek 11:20; 20:20; 28:26; 34:24,30-31; 36:28; 37:23; Hos 2:23; 12:9; 13:4; Joel 2:27; Zeph 3:17; Zech 13:9; 2Cor 6:16; Heb 8:10
[11] Joel 2:27 NASB
[12] Heb 11:16 NASB
[13] 1Cor 6:19 ESV

for Christ Jesus has made you His own.[14] Jesus has called you His friend.[15] Your body is a member of Christ.[16]

Baptized: Jesus Christ is in you.[17] You have been baptized[18] into Christ Jesus,[19] in the name of the Father and of the Son and of the Holy Spirit.[20] Through baptism you have put on Christ.[21] Baptism now saves you, not as a removal of dirt from the body but as an appeal to God for a good conscience, through the resurrection of Jesus Christ.[22] For since you have been united with Christ in a death like His, you will certainly also be united with Him in a resurrection like His.[23]

...Christ Jesus has made me His own.

Philippians 3:12 ESV

---

[14] Phil 3:12 ESV;
cf. Tit 2:14
[15] John 15:15 NASB;
cf. Jas 2:23
[16] 1Cor 6:15 NASB

[17] 2Cor 13:5 NASB;
cf. Rom 8:10;
Col 1:27
[18] Rom 6:3 NASB;
cf. Matt 28:19;
Gal 3:27

[19] Rom 6:3 NASB;
cf. Gal 3:27
[20] Matt 28:19 NKJV
[21] Gal 3:27 NKJV
[22] 1Pet 3:21 ESV
[23] Rom 6:5 NIV

Yesterday

10. Adopted into God's Family

Welcome to the family! What a gracious expression of inclusion and honor! Your relationship with God—Father, Son, and Holy Spirit—is far deeper and richer than any human analogy could ever express. But in His Word God compares your relationship with Him to that of a *child*, a *brother or sister*, an *heir*, and a *lover*. All of these roles provide helpful insights into the most amazing relationship since creation: the Father and His Son, Jesus, love you just as much as they love each other!

It's official: You have been adopted as God's child.[1] Jesus gave you the right to become God's child.[2] Through faith in Christ Jesus[3] you are a child of the Most High, the living God, the Lord Almighty.[4] You have received the Spirit of adoption,[5] and the Spirit Himself testifies with your spirit that you are God's child.[6] See what great love the Father has lavished on you, that you should be called a child of God! And that is what you are![7]

God's your Father: The Lord Almighty is your Father.[8] You acknowledge the Son and have the Father also.[9] God has sent forth the Spirit of His Son into your heart crying out, "Abba!* Father!"[10] You are God's child now,[11] and God treats you as His child.[12] The Lord has spared you as a man spares his own child who serves him.[13]

Christ's your Brother: God has given you, His child, to Jesus.[14] God called you into the fellowship of His Son, Jesus Christ our Lord;[15] Your fellowship is with the Father and with His Son Jesus Christ.[16] Jesus is not ashamed to call you His brother or sister.[17]

---

[1] Gal 4:5 ESV; cf. Eph 1:5; Rom 8:15
[2] John 1:12 NKJV
[3] Gal 3:26 NKJV
[4] Luke 6:35; Hos 1:10; Rom 9:26; 2Cor 6:18 NKJV; cf. Matt 5:9; Acts 17:28; Rom 8:14; Gal 3:26; 4:7
[5] Rom 8:15 NKJV; cf. Gal 4:5
[6] Rom 8:16 NASB
[7] 1John 3:1 NIV
[8] 2Cor 6:18 NKJV; cf. Deut 32:6; Is 64:8; Jer 31:9; Mal 2:10; Matt 6:9; Luke 11:2
[9] 1John 2:23 NKJV
[10] Gal 4:6 NKJV; cf. Rom 8:15
[11] 1John 3:2 NKJV
[12] Heb 12:7 NIV
[13] Mal 3:17 NKJV
[14] Heb 2:13 NKJV
[15] 1Cor 1:9 NKJV
[16] 1John 1:3 NKJV
[17] Heb 2:11 NIV; cf. Matt 12:50; Mark 3:35

Engaged to God: You call your Maker, the Lord of hosts, your Husband.[18] The Lord will betroth you to Himself[19] in righteousness, justice, steadfast love, mercy, and faithfulness forever.[20] God gave you the Spirit in your heart as a pledge**.[21]

Promised heir: You are a child of promise,[22] God's promised heir.[23] He chose you to be an heir of the promised kingdom[24] and has caused you to be born again[25] into an inheritance that can never perish, spoil, or fade. This inheritance is kept in heaven for you.[26] The Father has qualified you to share in the inheritance of the saints in Light.[27] The Spirit Himself testifies with your spirit that you are God's heir, and co-heir with Christ.[28]

> *Both the One who makes people holy and those who are made holy are of the same family. So Jesus is not ashamed to call them brothers and sisters.*
>
> *Hebrews 2:11 NIV*

---

[18] Is 54:5 NKJV;
  cf. Hos 2:16
[19] Hos 2:19 NKJV;
  cf. 2Cor 11:2
[20] Hos 2:19-20 ESV
[21] 2Cor 1:22 NASB
[22] Gal 4:28 NASB

[23] Rom 4:13 NASB;
  cf. Gal 4:7
[24] Jas 2:5 NASB;
  cf. Mark 10:14
[25] 1Pet 1:3 NASB
[26] 1Pet 1:4 NIV
[27] Col 1:12 NASB
[28] Rom 8:16-17 NIV

* See *Abba* in glossary.

** Consider the Holy Spirit in you to be your "engagement ring."

11. Assigned Special Roles

As a child of God, you are provided many special and significant roles here on earth and beyond. You did not earn these, but you received them as a part of God's gracious gift to you. He made you a *member*, or part, of His body—the fellowship of all believers. You are like a *sheep* under the Good Shepherd, guarded and guided by our Lord. God declared you His *priest*, tasked with sharing His love and message with believers and nonbelievers alike. He has planted you in this specific time and place to accomplish His gracious purposes and to extend His love. He truly enables you to bloom right where you are planted.

Member of Christ's body: You are part of the church of God.[1] You were baptized in one Spirit into one body.[2] You are a member of Christ's body,[3] and God arranged you in that body as He chose.[4] You have fellowship with fellow believers*.[5] You are part of God's building,[6] the temple of the living God.[7] Christ is faithful over God's house, of whose house you are a part.[8]

Sheep of the Good Shepherd: The Lord God is your Shepherd,[9] and you are a human sheep of God's pasture,[10] a sheep of His hand.[11] The Lord set over you one Shepherd,[12] Jesus Christ[13]—the Good Shepherd,[14] that great Shepherd of the sheep.[15]

Citizen of Christ's Kingdom: Know that Jesus Christ, the Lamb, made you part of His kingdom.[16] The Father rescued you from the domain of darkness and transferred you to the kingdom of His beloved Son.[17] The Lord has inherited you, one of His people, as His chosen portion and inheritance.[18] The Lord is your King; He will save you.[19]

---

[1] 1Cor 1:2 NASB
[2] 1Cor 12:13 ESV
[3] 1Cor 12:18 NASB;
cf. 1Cor 12:27
[4] 1Cor 12:18 ESV
[5] 1John 1:7 NASB
[6] 1Cor 3:9 NASB
[7] 2Cor 6:16 NASB
[8] Heb 3:6 NASB

[9] Ps 23:1 ESV;
cf. Ezek 34:15
[10] Ezek 34:31 ESV;
cf. Ps 79:13; 95:7;
100:3
[11] Ps 95:7 NASB
[12] Ezek 34:23 NASB
[13] Matt 2:6 NKJV
[14] John 10:11,14
NKJV

[15] Heb 13:20 NKJV
[16] Rev 5:10 NASB;
cf. Rev 1:6
[17] Col 1:13 NASB
[18] Zech 2:12;
Deut 32:9;
Ps 33:12 NIV
[19] Is 33:22 NASB

Priest to God: You are part of the Lord's kingdom of royal priests.[20] Jesus Christ made you a priest to His God and Father.[21]

Planted in the Lord's field: You are part of the Lord God's field,[22] His pleasant vineyard; He keeps His vineyard night and day.[23] The Lord sows you for Himself in the earth.[24]

Now you are the body of Christ and individually members of it.

1 Corinthians 12:27 ESV

---

[20] Ex 19:6;
   1Pet 2:9 NASB
[21] Rev 1:6 NASB;
   cf. Rev 5:10

[22] 1Cor 3:9 NASB
[23] Is 27:2 ESV
[24] Hos 2:23 NKJV

* *Literally,*
one another.

Yesterday

Those He Called, He Also Justified[1]

The "elephant in the room" is that your God is holy but you are not. He can't tolerate sin and you can't steer clear of it. This sounds like irreconcilable differences, but thankfully the story does not end there. The God who called you also took it upon Himself to *justify* you, which means He made you righteous before Him, just as if you had never sinned. This section explores all that went into your justification.

12. Received the Gift of God's Son

Jesus—a gift unlike any other! Only one thing stood in the way of God's desire for you to dwell with Him in love forever—your sin. God is holy, and He cannot coexist with sin or evil. Only perfect, sinless people can be a part of His kingdom. What you could never have done, God Himself did for you by sending Jesus to take upon Himself the punishment you deserved. The wages of your sin was death, both in time and eternity, but Jesus took your place. What an incredible gift at such a horrific price!

God's Son given: You know that the Son of God has come.[2] For to you a Child is born, to you a Son is given; and He is called Wonderful Counselor, Mighty God, Everlasting Father, Prince of Peace.[3] God gave His only Son,[4] Jesus Christ, who loves you and gave Himself for your sins.[5]

He took your sin: God, being compassionate,[6] atoned for you for all that you have done.[7] God sent His own Son in the likeness of sinful flesh to be a sin offering.[8] He made Him who had no sin to be sin for you.[9] The Lord has laid on Christ* your sin and iniquity,[10] which He

---

[1] Rom 8:30 NIV
[2] 1John 5:20 NIV
[3] Is 9:6 NIV
[4] John 3:16 ESV;
  cf. Rom 8:32

[5] Gal 2:20; 1:4
  NASB
[6] Ps 78:38 NASB
[7] Ezek 16:63 ESV;
  cf. Ps 78:38

[8] Rom 8:3-4 NIV
[9] 2Cor 5:21 NIV
[10] Is 53:6,11,12
  NKJV

bore for you.[11] For His own sake the Lord has blotted out your transgressions[12] like a cloud[13] and your sins[14] like mist.[15]

He died for you: By God's grace[16] Jesus Christ, our Lord, was delivered over to death for your sins,[17] the just for the unjust,[18] in accordance with the Scriptures.[19]

Once for all: Christ has appeared once for you at the end of the ages to put away your sin by the sacrifice of Himself.[20] By God's will Christ offered His body[21] and laid down His life for you,[22] and by a single offering Christ has perfected you[23] once for all.[24]

Your debt canceled: Surely Christ has borne your griefs and carried your sorrows.[25] He was pierced and stricken for your transgressions;[26] He was crushed for your iniquities; the punishment that brought you peace was on Him.[27] God has forgiven you all your trespasses, by canceling the record of debt that stood against you with its legal demands.[28]

"For God so loved the world, that He gave His only Son, that whoever believes in Him should not perish but have eternal life."

John 3:16 ESV

---

[11] Is 53:12 NKJV; cf. 1Pet 2:24
[12] Is 43:25 ESV; cf. Is 44:22
[13] Is 44:22 ESV
[14] Is 44:22 ESV; cf. Acts 3:19
[15] Is 44:22 ESV
[16] Heb 2:9 NIV
[17] Rom 4:25; 5:8 NIV; cf. Rom 14:15; 1Cor 8:11; 15:3; 2Cor 5:14; 1Thes 5:10; Heb 2:9
[18] 1Pet 3:18 NASB
[19] 1Cor 15:3 ESV
[20] Heb 9:26 ESV
[21] Heb 10:10 NASB
[22] 1John 3:16 NASB
[23] Heb 10:14 ESV; cf. Heb 9:28
[24] Heb 10:10 NKJV; cf. Heb 9:28; 1Pet 3:18
[25] Is 53:4 NKJV
[26] Is 53:5,8 ESV
[27] Is 53:5 NIV
[28] Col 2:13-14 ESV

* *Literally,* "My righteous Servant" —refers to the Messiah (Christ).

13. Christ Sacrificed Himself

Unlucky 13? Can you picture the devil and his cohorts glee-fully presuming Jesus to be extremely unlucky as He was being nailed to the cross? But in the most incredible turn-around in history, death could not hold Jesus, and His death ended up pay-ing in full everything that you owed. The Jewish Passover celebration, with its annual sacrifice of a spotless lamb and sprinkled blood, found its complete, once-for-all fulfillment in the astounding self-sacrifice of the perfect Lamb of God for you.

Your Priest: You have a great Priest over the house of God,[1] who is holy, innocent, unstained, separated from sinners, and exalted above the heavens.[2] Christ, as a merciful and faithful high priest in service to God, makes atonement for your sins.[3]

Your Sacrifice: God sent His Son, Jesus Christ,[4] who offered Himself once for all[5] as the atoning sacrifice for your sins, and not only for yours but also for the sins of the whole world.[6] Christ died for you,[7] and you are justified freely by God's grace through the redemption that came by Christ Jesus. God presented Christ as a sacrifice of atonement, through the shedding of His blood.[8] For the joy set before Him Jesus endured the cross for you, scorning its shame.[9]

Cleansed by His blood: Jesus Christ has freed you from your sins by His blood.[10] Jesus, God's Son, suffered to sanctify you through His own blood of the new covenant,[11] poured out for you for forgiveness of sins.[12] The blood of Jesus His Son cleanses you from all sin.[13] You have been sprinkled with[14] and justified by[15] Christ's blood.[16]

---

[1] Heb 10:21 NASB
[2] Heb 7:26 ESV
[3] Heb 2:17 NIV;
cf. Rom 3:25
[4] 1John 4:10 NIV
[5] Heb 7:27 NIV
[6] 1John 2:2 NIV;
cf. 1John 4:10

[7] Rom 5:8 NIV;
cf. Rom 14:15;
1Cor 8:11; 2Cor 5:14; 1Thes 5:10
[8] Rom 3:24-25 NIV
[9] Heb 12:2 NIV
[10] Rev 1:5 NIV
[11] Heb 13:12; Matt 26:28;

Luke 22:20;
Heb 10:29 NIV
[12] Matt 26:28 NASB;
cf. Luke 22:20
[13] 1John 1:7 NASB
[14] 1Pet 1:2 NASB
[15] Rom 5:9 NASB
[16] 1Pet 1:2; Rom 5:9 NASB

His body given for you: Christ's body has been given for you.[17] You enter the holy places by the new and living way that He opened for you through the curtain, that is, through His flesh.[18] By Christ's wounds you have been healed.[19]

... [Jesus] sacrificed for their sins once for all when He offered Himself.
Hebrews 7:27 NIV

---

[17] Luke 22:19 NASB
[18] Heb 10:19-20 ESV

[19] 1Pet 2:24 NIV;
cf. Is 53:5

14. Saved by Grace Through Faith

At a friend's wedding, his bride's mind went blank when she was to recite her vows. When he softly prompted her, "*love me and serve me*," she replied out loud, "love me and serve me." At the end, she hadn't actually promised him anything! In a sense, your vows to God are much like that. The forces of darkness—the devil, the evil world, and your sinful nature—are more powerful than you yourself could possibly overcome. And on your own you would never be able to escape God's righteous wrath over your sin. But thanks be to God, who sent His only Son, Jesus Christ, to do for you what you could never have done! You can't guarantee to God how loving and faithful *you* will be, but instead you can thank *Him* for His incredible gift of grace, and declare to Him how loving and faithful *He* is. Be assured that He will take it from there.

Saved from the wrath to come: God saved you because of His own mercy,[1] which he gave you in Christ Jesus before the ages began.[2] Jesus delivers you from the wrath to come.[3] For unto you was born in the city of David a Savior, who is Christ the Lord.[4] Now in the days of Christ the King*[5] you have been saved[6] by Christ's life[7] and dwell securely.[8] Christ saves you to the uttermost.[9]

Delivered from darkness: The Lord delivers your soul from death.[10] The Father has delivered you from the domain of darkness.[11] Jesus Christ delivered you from the present evil age, according to the will of your God and Father.[12]

Gifted with grace: The grace of God has appeared,[13] and by this grace[14] you have been saved[15] through faith in the Lord Jesus Christ.[16]

[1] Tit 3:5; 2Tim 1:9 NIV
[2] 2Tim 1:9; Tit 3:6 ESV
[3] 1Thes 1:10 NKJV
[4] Luke 2:11 ESV
[5] Jer 23:5 NKJV; cf. Jer 30:9; 33:14-15,17
[6] Jer 33:16 NKJV; cf. Jer 23:6; John 3:17; Acts 4:12; Rom 5:10; 10:13
[7] Rom 5:10 NKJV
[8] Jer 33:16 ESV
[9] Heb 7:25 NKJV
[10] Ps 116:8 NKJV
[11] Col 1:13 ESV
[12] Gal 1:4 NKJV
[13] Tit 2:11 NKJV
[14] Eph 2:8 NKJV; cf. Acts 15:11; 2Tim 1:9; Tit 2:11
[15] Eph 2:8 NKJV; cf. Acts 15:11; 16:31; Rom 10:9-10; 2Tim 1:9; Tit 2:11
[16] Eph 2:8; Acts 16:31 NKJV; cf. Rom 10:9-10

And this is not your own doing; it is the gift of God, not a result of your works, so that you may not boast.[17]

All by the Word of truth: Of His own will, the Father[18] has given you life[19] by the Word of truth.[20] The Gospel, the word of the cross, is the power of God to you[21] for salvation.[22] Jesus Christ gave knowledge of salvation to you in the forgiveness of your sins.[23] God's implanted word has saved your soul.[24]

For by grace you have been saved through faith, and that not of yourselves; it is the gift of God.
Ephesians 2:8 NKJV

---

[17] Eph 2:8-9 ESV
[18] Jas 1:18 NKJV
[19] Ps 119:93 NKJV
[20] Jas 1:18 NKJV; cf. Ps 119:93
[21] Rom 1:16 NASB; cf. 1Cor 1:18
[22] Rom 1:16 NASB
[23] Luke 1:77 ESV
[24] Jas 1:21 NKJV

* *Literally,* "Branch of righteousness," "raise(d) to David," "King"—referring to the promised Messiah (Christ).

15. Forgiven

> You've probably watched a movie or two in which a "not guilty" verdict left people cheering and hugging. Perhaps you have even experienced something like this in real life. With God as your Judge and Jesus as your defense attorney, your acquittal is certain. God truly forgives you in Christ and forgets your sins. And there is a lot of cheering and hugging in heaven every time another sinner repents and is declared *not guilty*.[1]

God's compassion: The Lord your God is a compassionate God,[2] and you have received mercy.[3] The Most High God is kind[4] and gracious to you,[5] and has dealt bountifully with you.[6] As a father shows compassion to His children,[7] so the Lord shows compassion to you[8] with everlasting love.[9] In God's great compassion He does not make an end of you or forsake you,[10] for the Lord is a gracious and compassionate God.[11] He will not withhold His compassion from you,[12] but exalts Himself to show mercy to you.[13] The mercy of the Lord Jesus Christ leads to eternal life.[14]

Sins forgiven: The Lord God is compassionate and merciful toward your iniquities and has atoned for them.[15] The Lord deals with you for His name's sake,[16] not according to your sins,[17] your evil ways, or your corrupt deeds.[18] Know that Jesus, your Leader and Savior, gave repentance to you,[19] abundantly pardons you,[20] and saves you from your sins.[21] For Christ's sake[22] and through His name,[23] the Lord God, your

---

[1] Luke 15:7
[2] Deut 4:31 NASB; cf. Ex 34:6; Hos 2:23
[3] Hos 2:1 ESV; cf. Matt 5:7; Luke 1:50; 6:36; 1Pet 2:10
[4] Luke 6:35 NKJV; cf. Tit 3:4
[5] Is 30:18 NKJV; cf. Ex 34:6
[6] Ps 13:6 NKJV
[7] Ps 103:13 ESV
[8] Ps 103:13 ESV; cf. Is 54:8,10; 55:7; Micah 7:19
[9] Is 54:8 ESV
[10] Neh 9:31 NASB; cf. Deut 4:31
[11] Neh 9:31 NASB; cf. Jonah 4:2
[12] Ps 40:11 NASB
[13] Is 30:18 ESV
[14] Jude 1:21 ESV
[15] Ps 78:38; Heb 8:12 ESV
[16] Ezek 20:44 NASB
[17] Ps 103:10 NASB
[18] Ezek 20:44 NASB
[19] Acts 5:31 ESV
[20] Is 55:7 NKJV
[21] Matt 1:21 NKJV
[22] 1John 2:12 NKJV
[23] Acts 10:43 NKJV

Father, forgives you your sins[24] and trespasses,[25] passes over your transgression,[26] and takes away your iniquity.[27]

Sins forgotten: The Lord covers all your sin,[28] and He remembers your sins and your lawless deeds no more.[29] None of the transgressions which you have committed shall be remembered against you.[30] The Lord treads your sins underfoot and hurls all your iniquities into the depths of the sea.[31] As far as the east is from the west, so far has the Lord has removed your transgressions from you.[32]

> "...To [Jesus] all the prophets bear witness that everyone who believes in Him receives forgiveness of sins through His name."
> Acts 10:43 ESV

---

[24] 1John 1:9;
Luke 1:77;
Col 1:14 NKJV;
cf. Matt 1:21; Acts
5:31; 10:43; Eph
1:7; 1John 2:12
[25] Mark 11:25 NKJV

[26] Micah 7:18 NKJV
[27] Zech 3:4 ESV;
cf. Ps 32:5; 85:2;
103:3; Is 33:24;
Jer 31:34;
Micah 7:18
[28] Ps 85:2 ESV

[29] Heb 10:17 ESV;
cf. Is 43:25; Jer
31:34; Heb 8:12
[30] Ezek 18:22 NKJV
[31] Micah 7:19 NIV
[32] Ps 103:12 NIV

16. Redeemed by God

Perhaps you have heard the tale of a boy who builds his own toy boat, only to lose it to a sudden river surge. Weeks later he finds his boat for sale in a resale shop, and does extra work for people until he has enough money to buy his boat back. He then declares the boat "twice his." With God, you are likewise *twice His*—first *created* by Him, and later *redeemed* (bought back) by Him. You have been redeemed from you sins and from the curse of the Law, and now you are fully forgiven. God paid an exorbitant price to get you back at all costs.

Your Redeemer lives: The Holy One, the God of all the earth, is your Redeemer.[1] In His love and mercy He redeemed you.[2] In Christ Jesus[3] He has redeemed[4] your life[5] with His arm[6] to be one of His people.[7] You are among those called "The Redeemed of the Lord."[8] You know that your Redeemer lives, and at the last He will stand upon the earth.[9]

Redeemed from sins: The Lord, with whom there is plentiful redemption, has redeemed you from all your iniquities.[10] Christ redeemed you from the curse of the law by becoming a curse for you—for it is written, "Cursed is everyone who is hanged on a tree."[11] He redeemed you[12] through His blood[13] from every lawless deed and purified you.[14] In the Father's beloved Son you have redemption, the forgiveness of sins.[15]

Ransomed by God: You are among the ransomed of the Lord.[16] He bought you with a price.[17] The Son of Man did not come to be served but to serve,[18] and to give his life as a ransom for you.[19] By His precious blood the Lamb ransomed you for God.[20]

---

[1] Is 54:5 NIV; *cf.* Is 44:24; 49:26; 54:8
[2] Is 63:9 NIV
[3] Rom 3:24 NASB
[4] Is 43:1 NASB; *cf.* Ex 15:13; Ps 34:22; 111:9; Is 44:23; Luke 1:68; Rom 3:24; Gal 4:5
[5] Ps 34:22 ESV
[6] Ps 77:15 NKJV
[7] 1Chron 17:21 ESV
[8] Is 62:12 NASB
[9] Job 19:25 ESV
[10] Ps 130:7-8 ESV
[11] Gal 3:13 ESV
[12] Tit 2:14 NASB; *cf.* Eph 1:7
[13] Eph 1:7 NASB
[14] Tit 2:14 NASB
[15] Col 1:14 NASB
[16] Is 35:10; 51:11 NASB
[17] 1Cor 6:20; 7:23 NASB; *cf.* Ex 15:16
[18] Matt 20:28 NASB
[19] Matt 20:28 NIV; *cf.* 1Tim 2:6
[20] Rev 5:9; 1Pet 1:18-19 ESV

..."Do not fear, for I have redeemed you; I have called you by name; you are Mine!"

Isaiah 43:1 NASB

17. Made Right with God

To *account* something as true is not a matter of wishing or pretending. Accounting pertains to carefully balanced books. It is seeing a situation as it really is. A person is accounted debt free, not just based on hope or positive thinking, but when confirmed by facts: no outstanding student loans, no mortgage or car payments, etc. God declares you "sin free" for the sake of Christ. He accounts you righteous and blameless, and you can bank on that!

Justified: God justified you[1] by faith through your Lord Jesus Christ[2] as a gift by His grace.[3] Christ's act of righteousness[4] and His resurrection[5] led to your justification[6] in the name of the Lord Jesus Christ and by the Spirit of our God.[7] God makes you worthy of His calling,[8] and you are considered worthy of the kingdom of God.[9]

Accounted righteous: By His knowledge the Righteous One, God's Servant, made you to be accounted righteous[10] apart from works of the law.[11] The free gift[12] of God's righteousness[13] through faith[14] in Jesus Christ[15] is for you.[16] The Law and the Prophets bear witness to this.[17] By sending His own Son in the likeness of sinful flesh and for sin, God condemned sin in the flesh, in order that the righteous requirement of the law might be fulfilled in you.[18] He is the God of your righteousness.[19] You believed God, and it was accounted to you for righteousness.[20] He has made you righteous[21] and your way blameless.[22]

---

[1] Rom 8:30 NASB; cf. Is 45:25; Rom 3:24,26; 4:25; 5:1,15-16,18; 8:33; 1Cor 6:11; Gal 2:16; 3:24; Tit 3:7
[2] Rom 5:1 NASB; cf. Rom 3:26; Gal 2:16; 3:24
[3] Rom 3:24 NASB; cf. Tit 3:7
[4] Rom 5:18 NASB
[5] Rom 4:25 NASB
[6] Rom 5:18 ESV; cf. Rom 4:25; 5:16; 1Cor 6:11
[7] 1Cor 6:11 ESV
[8] 2Thes 1:11 ESV
[9] 2Thes 1:5 NASB
[10] Is 53:11 ESV; cf. Rom 4:6,11,24
[11] Rom 3:20-21 NASB; cf. Rom 4:6
[12] Rom 5:17 ESV
[13] Rom 3:22 NASB; cf. Ps 103:17; Rom 5:17; Phil 3:9
[14] Rom 3:22 NASB; cf. Phil 3:9
[15] Rom 3:22 NASB; cf. Rom 5:17; Phil 3:9
[16] Rom 3:22 NASB
[17] Rom 3:21 ESV
[18] Rom 8:3-4 ESV
[19] Ps 4:1 NKJV
[20] Jas 2:23 NKJV
[21] Rom 5:19 NKJV
[22] Ps 18:32 NASB

Righteousness abounds: In Christ you have become the righteousness of God.[23] As God's righteous one, you live by faith.[24] Having received the abundance of grace and the free gift of righteousness, you reign in life through Jesus Christ.[25] You serve the Lord without fear, in righteousness before Him all your days,[26] and you are exalted in the Lord's righteousness.[27] In you, grace reigns through righteousness leading to eternal life through Jesus Christ your Lord.[28]

...by [Jesus Christ's] obedience the many will be made righteous.

Romans 5:19 ESV

---

[23] 2Cor 5:21 ESV;
   cf. Jer 23:6; 33:16

[24] Heb 10:38 NASB;
   cf. Gal 3:11

[25] Rom 5:17 ESV

[26] Luke 1:74-75 ESV

[27] Ps 89:16 NKJV

[28] Rom 5:21 ESV

18. Made Holy and Blameless

> Saint _____? (Fill in *your* name.) God invites you
> to trade in the filthy rags of your own self-righteousness for the
> radiant-white robe of Christ's righteousness. He declares you
> clean, and calls you His saint, His "holy one." *Saint* means one
> who has been deliberately set apart for a special purpose. If you
> have a jersey you always wear during games of your favorite
> sports team, that jersey is *holy* to you. To God, everything
> about you is special and holy. He has declared you so. Thanks
> to Christ you are now in fact His *saint*!

Chosen to be holy: God chose you in Christ,[1] who presents you holy
and blameless and above reproach before Him.[2] You are among those
called "The Holy People."[3]

Washed clean: Through Christ's sacrificial death a fountain has been
opened for you, to cleanse you from sin and impurity.[4] The Lord God
has sprinkled clean water on you,[5] and you have been cleansed from
all your filthiness.[6] He has cleansed you[7] from all your sinful backsliding[8] and from all your idols.[9] By faith[10] your heart has been sprinkled
clean[11] from an evil conscience and your body has been washed with
pure water.[12] You were washed, you were sanctified, you were justified in the name of the Lord Jesus Christ and by the Spirit of our God.[13]
This is a trustworthy saying: God saved you through the washing of
rebirth and renewal by the Holy Spirit.[14] You confess your sins, and
God is faithful and just to forgive you your sins and to cleanse you
from all unrighteousness.[15] Jesus has already made you clean because
of the word He has spoken to you.[16]

Given the robe of righteousness: The Lord God has clothed and
adorned you with the garments of salvation.[17] Though your sins were

[1] Eph 1:4 NASB
[2] Col 1:22 ESV; cf. Eph 1:4
[3] Is 62:12 NIV
[4] Zech 13:1 NIV
[5] Ezek 36:25 NASB
[6] Ezek 36:25 NASB; cf. Ezek 36:33; Zech 13:1
[7] Ezek 36:25 NASB; cf. Ezek 37:23
[8] Ezek 37:23 NIV
[9] Ezek 36:25 NASB
[10] Acts 15:9 NASB
[11] Heb 10:22 NASB; cf. Acts 15:9
[12] Heb 10:22 ESV
[13] 1Cor 6:11 NIV
[14] Tit 3:5-6,8 NIV
[15] 1John 1:9 NKJV
[16] John 15:3 NIV
[17] Is 61:10 ESV; cf. Ps 149:4

like scarlet, they are as white as snow; though they were red like crimson, they have become like wool.[18] The Lord God has covered you with the robe of righteousness as a bridegroom decks himself like a priest with a beautiful headdress, and as a bride adorns herself with her jewels.[19]

Purified: Our great God and Savior Jesus Christ gave Himself for you to purify you and make you zealous for good works.[20] The Lord anoints[21] and sanctifies you[22] in the name of the Lord Jesus Christ[23] by the Spirit of our God.[24] By God's will you have been made holy through the sacrifice of the body of Jesus Christ once for all.[25] You are a saint of the Most High,[26] and you serve the Lord in holiness before Him all the days of your life.[27]

> [Christ] has now reconciled [you] in His body of flesh by His death, in order to present you holy and blameless and above reproach before Him.
>
> Colossians 1:22 ESV

---

[18] Is 1:18 NASB
[19] Is 61:10 ESV
[20] Tit 2:14 ESV
[21] 2Cor 1:21 NKJV
[22] Lev 20:8 NKJV; *cf.* Lev 21:8; 22:32; Ezek 37:28;

1Cor 1:30; 6:11; 1Pet 1:2
[23] 1Cor 6:11 ESV
[24] 1Cor 6:11 ESV; *cf.* 1Pet 1:2
[25] Heb 10:10 NIV
[26] Dan 7:18,27 NKJV;

cf. Ps 31:23; 34:9; Rom 1:7; 1Cor 1:2; 6:1-2; Col 1:12; Rev 14:12
[27] Luke 1:74-75 NKJV

19. At Peace with God

When someone close to you is disappointed, upset, or angry with you, life can become stressful and unpleasant. Tensions may mount and a dark cloud may hover over you. Are you sometimes keenly aware of your failures before God and how you have repeatedly disappointed Him?   Such realizations might lead you to promise to try harder next time, or to justify yourself and make excuses, or just to give up and try to hide from Him. You might even wonder if you have sinned against God one-too-many times, leaving you uncertain of His ongoing love and approval. The amazing truth is that in love Christ died for you, to take your place and to pay in full for every one of those sins. In Christ no condemnation or judgment remains. Be reassured that God loves you perfectly, and He enables nothing less than perfect peace for you in your relationship with Him. So long, dark cloud!

In perfect peace: You have peace with God[1] through your Lord Jesus Christ.[2] Through Christ the Father has reconciled you to Himself, having made peace by the blood of His cross.[3] The Lord's covenant of peace shall not be removed from you.[4] Jesus gives you rest for your soul.[5] You trust in the Lord, and He keeps you in perfect peace.[6] His perfect love casts out your fear.[7]

Reconciled to God: Christ has reconciled you to God[8] in His fleshly body through death.[9] In Christ Jesus you have been brought near by the blood of Christ.[10] There is no condemnation for you,[11] as the Lord has taken away His judgments against you.[12] The law of the Spirit of life has set you free in Christ Jesus from the law of sin and death.[13]

---

[1] Rom 5:1 NASB;
  cf. Num 6:26
[2] Rom 5:1 NASB
[3] Col 1:20 NASB
[4] Is 54:10 ESV
[5] Matt 11:28-29 NASB

[6] Is 26:3 NASB
[7] 1John 4:18 NASB
[8] Col 1:22; Rom 5:10-11 NASB;
  cf. 2Cor 5:19
[9] Col 1:22 NASB;
  cf. Rom 5:10-11

[10] Eph 2:13 NASB
[11] Rom 8:1 NASB;
  cf. Ps 34:22
[12] Zeph 3:15 NASB
[13] Rom 8:2 ESV

Therefore, having been justified by faith, we have peace with God through our Lord Jesus Christ,

Romans 5:1 NASB

Those He Justified, He Also Glorified [1]

You are a new creation; the old has passed away and the new has come. You are being transformed from darkness into brilliant light. All will one day marvel at everything God has done for you and accomplished through you.

20. Old Self Died

> Your new life begins with your death! Your old, sinful nature, inherited from your original parents, Adam and Eve, cannot be reformed or rehabilitated. It must instead be put to death. It does no good to dress your old self in formal wear; it must be completely done away with. Self-help books are useful for various aspects of life, but when it comes to your sinful nature and being right with God, self-help can only make things worse. God has provided you the only viable solution. Since you by faith have participated in Christ's death, your slavery to sin has been ended, the claims of the Law on you have been set aside, and your heart of stone has been removed. Since you died with Him, you will most certainly...well, after you are finished with this topic, kindly proceed to the next!

Crucified with Christ: Because of God [2] you are in Christ Jesus. [3] The old has passed away. [4] You have been buried with Christ Jesus through baptism into death. [5] Christ has died for you; [6] therefore you have died with Him, [7] and your life is hidden with Him in God. [8] You share Jesus' sufferings, becoming like Him in His death. [9] Jesus Christ our Lord has delivered you from your body of death. [10]

Freed from sin: Through God's promises you have escaped the corruption in the world caused by evil desires. [11] Your old self was crucified with Christ, [12] so that the body ruled by sin might be done

---

[1] Rom 8:30 NIV
[2] 1Cor 1:30 ESV
[3] 1Cor 1:30 ESV;
 cf. 2Cor 5:17
[4] 2Cor 5:17 ESV
[5] Rom 6:4 NASB;
 cf. Col 2:12

[6] Rom 5:6,8 NASB;
 cf. Rom 14:15-16;
 1Cor 8:11;
 2Cor 5:14
[7] 2Cor 5:14; Rom 6:8
 ESV; *cf.* Rom 6:5;
 Col 3:3; 2Tim 2:11

[8] Col 3:3 NKJV
[9] Phil 3:10 ESV
[10] Rom 7:24-25
 NKJV
[11] 2Pet 1:4 NIV
[12] Rom 6:6 NIV;
 cf. Gal 2:20

away with, that you should no longer be a slave to sin.[13] Christ Himself bore your sins in His body on the cross,[14] so that you might die to sin.[15] Since you have died,[16] you have been set free from sin.[17]

Dead to the Law: You have died to the law[18] through the body of Christ, so that you may belong to Another, to Christ who has been raised from the dead.[19] For He is the end of the law for righteousness to you.[20]

Heart of stone removed: The Lord God has removed from you your heart of stone.[21]

For we know that our old self was crucified with Him so that the body ruled by sin might be done away with, that we should no longer be slaves to sin —

Romans 6:6 NIV

---

[13] Rom 6:6 NIV
[14] 1Pet 2:24 NASB
[15] 1Pet 2:24 NASB; cf. Rom 6:11
[16] Rom 6:7 NASB
[17] Rom 6:7,18,22 NIV
[18] Rom 7:4 ESV; cf. Gal 2:19
[19] Rom 7:4 ESV
[20] Rom 10:4 NASB
[21] Ezek 11:19 NIV; cf. Ezek 36:26

21. New Self Created

Perhaps at times you may feel that little about you has actually changed. You look the same in the mirror, and you tend to give in to many of the same temptations. But God wants you to know for a fact that the changes He has worked in you are very real and are critical for your life today and into eternity. Since you have died with Christ, so also you have been made alive with Him. You are, in fact, a new creation—in the process of being conformed to Jesus. You have been reborn and have been given a new heart and spirit, designed to align with God's own heart. You have been enabled to bear genuine fruit for Him. The old has indeed passed away, and all things have become new for you. Please know that God's Word is far more accurate and dependable than your feelings or perceptions could ever be!

New creation: You are in Christ,[1] and you are a new creation.[2] Behold, the new has come.[3] Your new self was created after the likeness of God in true righteousness and holiness.[4] Of His own will, the Father of lights brought you forth by the word of truth, that you should be a kind of firstfruits of His creatures.[5] You bear the image of the Man of heaven.[6]

New birth: Praise be to the God and Father of our Lord Jesus Christ! In His great mercy,[7] He has caused you to be born again[8] of imperishable seed, through the living and enduring word of God.[9] You have been born again[10] into a living hope through the resurrection of Jesus Christ from the dead.[11]

New heart: The Lord God has put a new spirit within you,[12] and your spirit has been made perfect.[13] He has given you a new heart, a heart of flesh.[14] The Lord your God has circumcised your heart, so that you may love Him with all your heart and with all your soul.[15] He put His

---

[1] 2Cor 5:17 NKJV
[2] 2Cor 5:17 NKJV; cf. Gal 6:15
[3] 2Cor 5:17 ESV
[4] Eph 4:24 ESV
[5] Jas 1:18 ESV
[6] 1Cor 15:49 ESV
[7] 1Pet 1:3 NIV
[8] 1Pet 1:3 NASB; cf. 1Pet 1:23
[9] 1Pet 1:23 NASB
[10] 1Pet 1:23 NASB; cf. 1Pet 1:3
[11] 1Pet 1:3 NIV
[12] Ezek 11:19 NKJV; cf. Ezek 36:26
[13] Heb 12:23 NKJV
[14] Ezek 36:26 NIV; cf. Ezek 11:19
[15] Deut 30:6 NIV

laws into your mind and wrote them on your heart.[16] You are God's workmanship, created in Christ Jesus for good works, which God prepared beforehand so that you would walk in them.[17] Christ chose you and appointed you so that you might go and bear fruit—fruit that will last.[18] The Lord has put the fear of Himself in your heart so that you will not turn away from Him.[19]

*I will give you a new heart
and put a new spirit in you....
Ezekiel 36:26 NIV*

---

[16] Heb 8:10 NASB;
   cf. Ps 37:31;

Jer 31:33;
Heb 10:16
[17] Eph 2:10 NASB

[18] John 15:16 NIV
[19] Jer 32:40 NASB

22. Living Through Christ

One day I was driving around a business campus in a distant city, searching for the building where training was to take place. I finally just walked into one of the buildings and asked the receptionist for directions to my destination. She replied, "Sir, you are in it." Do you ever find yourself searching for something that helps make your Christian experience more vibrant, more authentic, more meaningful, or more effective? If only you could figure out what was lacking, life might be so much better. Great news! In Christ the new you has already been infused with true life, and you have been fully empowered to become and do all God has planned for you. You have been set free to serve God without fear. His Spirit lives in you and is with you every moment of every day. There is no need to search anymore, because in Christ you are already right where you need to be.

Alive to God: Christ Jesus abolished death for you.[1] God sent His only Son into the world, so that you might live through Him.[2] Christ's act of righteousness has led to life for you.[3] You died to sin[4] and to the Law,[5] and you now live to God[6] in Christ Jesus.[7] By grace God has made you alive together with Christ.[8] In baptism you were raised with Christ through faith in the powerful working of God, who raised Him from the dead.[9] The Spirit of Him who raised Jesus from the dead is living in you, and He who raised Christ from the dead will also give life to your mortal body because of His Spirit who lives in you.[10] The life you now live in the body,[11] you live by faith in the Son of God.[12]

Alive to righteousness: You died with Christ, and so you also live with Him.[13] Since He is in you, although your body is dead because of sin, the Spirit is life because of righteousness.[14] Christ bore your sins in His body on the cross, so that you might live to righteousness.[15] You

---

[1] 2Tim 1:10 NASB
[2] 1John 4:9 ESV
[3] Rom 5:18 ESV
[4] Rom 6:11 NASB
[5] Gal 2:19 NASB

[6] Gal 2:19 NASB;
   cf. Luke 20:38;
   Rom 6:11
[7] Rom 6:11 NASB
[8] Eph 2:5 NASB;
   cf. Col 2:13
[9] Col 2:12 ESV

[10] Rom 8:11 NIV
[11] Gal 2:20 NIV
[12] Gal 2:20 NASB;
   cf. Hab 2:4
[13] Rom 6:8 NASB
[14] Rom 8:10 ESV
[15] 1Pet 2:24 NASB

have been set free from sin[16] and have become a slave of righteousness[17] and God's servant.[18] The Lord rules over you.[19] You will serve the Lord without fear, in righteousness before Him all the days of your life.[20]

In this the Love of God was made manifest among us, that God sent His only Son into the world, so that we might live through Him.

1 John 4:9 ESV

---

[16] Rom 6:22 NKJV;
  cf. Rom 6:7,18
[17] Rom 6:18 NASB

[18] Is 41:9 NASB;
  cf. Is 44:21;
  Rom 6:22

[19] 1Chron 29:12
  NASB
[20] Luke 1:74-75
  NKJV

23. **Into His Marvelous Light**

In Christ you are perfectly loved and completely forgiven. God has accomplished everything for you, and all is now fully in place. Christ has given you new, unending life, and He is perfectly capable of building upon the foundation that He has established in you. The Lord has provided you with everything you will need to effectively live out the adventure He's prepared for you.

Glorified: God glorified you,[1] and you glory in the Lord.[2] He called you out of darkness into His marvelous light.[3] You are a child of the light and a child of the day.[4] By grace God has seated you with Him in the heavenly places in Christ Jesus.[5]

Given every good thing: God, who did not spare his own Son, but gave Him up for you—how will He not also, along with Him, graciously give you all things?[6] You know every good thing that is in you for the sake of Christ.[7] You have a better possession and an abiding one,[8] and you have received a kingdom that cannot be shaken.[9]

Eternal life now: God has given you eternal life, and this life is in His Son. Since you have the Son, you have life.[10] You shall surely live; you shall not die.[11] You have passed out of death into life.[12] God so loved you, that He gave His only Son, that you should not perish but have eternal life.[13]

---

[1] Rom 8:30 NASB
[2] Is 45:25 NASB
[3] 1Pet 2:9 NASB
[4] 1Thes 5:5 NIV; *cf.* Eph 5:8
[5] Eph 2:5-6 NASB
[6] Rom 8:32 NIV
[7] Phm 1:6 NASB
[8] Heb 10:34 ESV
[9] Heb 12:28 NIV
[10] 1John 5:11-12 NIV
[11] Ezek 18:21 NIV
[12] John 5:24; 1John 3:14 NASB
[13] John 3:16 ESV

*You are all children of the light
and children of the day...*
1 Thessalonians 5:5 NIV

Standing firmly upon the solid base of God's *yesterday* promises and assurances, you are now warmly invited to explore and savor the amazing world of God's *today* promises and assurances for you!

That You May Know

TODAY

You know what is the immeasurable greatness
of God's power toward you.[1]

In his book "The Rest of the Gospel," coauthored with David Gregory, Dan Stone compares his experience of life as a Christian to a bed—with the *yesterday* facts about Christ's sacrifice like a sturdy headboard and the *forever* promises of eternal life like a solid footboard. But God's *today* assurances in his daily life had seemed to Dan more like a soggy, lumpy mattress. Can you identify? The reality is that God is just as active, engaged, and purposeful in your life now as He was during Christ's resurrection and as He will be in at Christ's glorious return. That exact same power is at work in you today!

Perhaps you are uneasy about His striking promises and assurances for your life right now. Maybe you fear that they are too good to be true or you judge yourself unworthy of them. Or possibly you are afraid to really bank on such promises. What if it they don't come true or what if your faith isn't strong enough? If it just depended on you, you would have genuine reason for concern. And not just you, but everyone other than Jesus who has ever walked this planet.

God winsomely invites you into the incredible adventure of life in and with Him in the here-and-now. The following assurances were not just written for others; they are written for *you*. God wants you to treasure and experience all He has for you. Are you ready to trade in that old mattress?

---

[1] Eph 1:18-19 ESV

Today

You Are God's Beloved

Why does God provide you so many promises and assurances? I am convinced it is because God is both the source and essence of love, and He so much wants you to know and experience that love. Following is a special opportunity for you to delight in several aspects of His amazing love for you today.

24. God Loves You Dearly

Let's start by trading in some lies you may have told yourself. Perhaps you have felt like you are a marginal, insignificant Christian. Maybe you doubt you will ever amount to much, or that God has any significant plans for your life. Well, guess again! The amazing truth is that you are greatly loved, intimately known, dearly accepted, and richly blessed by your Lord. What wonderful plans He has for your life! All He accomplishes in and through you will be celebrated throughout eternity!

Greatly loved: The Lord loves you[1] greatly[2] with everlasting love.[3] As the Father loves Jesus,[4] so Jesus[5] and His Father[6] love you.[7] The Lord allures you and speaks tenderly to you.[8] You have come to know and believe that love.[9]

Intimately known: The Lord God knows you,[10] and you are continually before Him.[11] The Lord searches you[12] and knows your days.[13] He

[1] Eph 2:4 NASB; cf. Ps 127:2; 146:8; Prov 3:12; Is 54:8; Jer 31:3; Zeph 3:17; Rom 5:5; 8:37,39; 9:25; 2Cor 13:11; Eph 1:4; 2Thes 2:13; 3:5; 1John 2:5; 4:16
[2] Eph 2:4 NASB
[3] Jer 31:3 NASB; cf. Is 54:8
[4] John 15:9 NASB;
cf. John 17:23
[5] John 15:9 NASB; cf. John 13:34; 14:21; Rom 8:37; Eph 3:19; 2Thes 2:16; Rev 3:19
[6] John 16:27 NASB; cf. John 14:21,23; 17:23; 2Thes 2:16; 1John 3:1
[7] John 15:9 NASB; cf. John 13:34; 14:21,23; 16:27; 17:23; Rom 8:37;
Eph 3:19; 2Thes 2:16; 1John 3:1; Rev 3:19
[8] Hos 2:14 NIV
[9] 1John 4:16 ESV
[10] 2Tim 2:19 NASB; cf. Ps 139:1; Jer 12:3; John 10:14,27; 1Cor 8:3; Gal 4:9
[11] Is 49:16 NASB
[12] Ps 139:1 NASB
[13] Ps 37:18 NASB

58

perceives your thoughts from afar.[14] Even before a word is on your tongue, the Lord knows it altogether.[15] He searches out your path[16] and is intimately acquainted with all your ways.[17] The Lord knows when you sit down, when you rise up,[18] and when you lie down.[19] Why, even the hairs of your head are all numbered![20]

Dearly accepted: Christ accepted you.[21] God is for you[22] and meets you in His steadfast love.[23] You are accepted by God[24]—a pleasing aroma to Him.[25] The Son of Man acknowledges you before the angels of God.[26] Whether you live or die,[27] you belong to Christ,[28] who was raised from the dead.[29]

Richly blessed: You trust in the Lord[30] and He blesses you.[31] You are called blessed upon the earth.[32] The Lord bestows His favor, honor,[33] and blessing on you.[34]

May the Lord direct your hearts to the love of God and to the steadfastness of Christ.
2 Thessalonians 3:5 ESV

---

[14] Ps 139:2 NIV
[15] Ps 139:4 ESV
[16] Ps 139:3 ESV
[17] Ps 139:3 NASB;
    cf. Ps 1:6
[18] Ps 139:2 NASB
[19] Ps 139:3 NASB
[20] Luke 12:7 ESV
[21] Rom 15:7 NASB
[22] Ps 56:9 NASB

[23] Ps 59:10 ESV
[24] Acts 10:35 NKJV;
    cf. Ezek 20:41
[25] Ezek 20:41 ESV
[26] Luke 12:8 NIV
[27] Rom 14:8 NIV
[28] Rom 7:4 NIV;
    cf. Rom 8:9;
    14:8-9; 2Tim 2:19
[29] Rom 7:4 NIV

[30] Jer 17:7 NASB
[31] Ps 5:12 NASB;
    cf. Ps 115:12-13;
    Is 61:9; Jer 17:7
[32] Ps 41:2 NASB
[33] Ps 84:11 NIV
[34] Is 44:3 NASB

25. Immanuel—God Is With You

How would you define *religion*? Some may see it as a system of beliefs and traditions, a philosophy of life and behavior, or an elevated state of mind. But when God promised the coming of Jesus the Messiah, He introduced Him as *Immanuel*—the God that is with you. God is so much more than a concept or ideal. God is not an *it,* but rather a *He. He* has come to be with you, *He* sent His Son to die for you, and *He* desires to develop an intimate, vibrant relationship with you. You are always on His mind. He dearly desires to be on yours as well.

Mutually abiding: Jesus and His Father have come to you.[1] You abide in the Father[2] and in the Son[3] and His love.[4] You know that[5] God abides in you[6] by the Spirit He gave you.[7]

God is with you: The virgin conceived and gave birth to a Son for you, and He is called Immanuel (which means "God with us").[8] The Lord your God,[9] the God of hosts,[10] the God of love[11] and peace,[12] declares that He[13] is continually[14] with you[15] wherever you go.[16] The Lord is with you to save you.[17] Jesus Christ is with you always, even to the end of the age,[18] and you live with our Lord Jesus Christ[19] because of the power of God directed toward you.[20]

[1] John 14:23 NASB; cf. Zech 2:10
[2] 1John 2:24 NASB; cf. 1John 3:24; 4:13,15,16
[3] 1John 2:24 NASB; cf. John 6:56; 15:5
[4] John 15:9 NASB
[5] 1John 4:13 NASB; cf. 1John 3:24
[6] 1John 3:24 NASB; cf. John 6:56; 15:5; 1John 2:24; 4:13,15,16
[7] 1John 3:24 NIV; cf. 1John 4:13
[8] Matt 1:23 NIV cf. Is 7:14
[9] Ezek 34:30 NASB; cf. Josh 1:9; Ps 46:7,11; Is 41:10; Amos 5:14
[10] Ps 46:7,11 NASB; cf. Amos 5:14
[11] 2Cor 13:11 NASB
[12] 2Cor 13:11 NASB; cf. 2Thes 3:16
[13] Hag 1:13 NASB
[14] Ps 73:23 NASB; cf. Matt 28:20
[15] Ps 23:4 NASB; cf. Gen 28:15;
Deut 31:8; Josh 1:5,9; Ps 14:5; 46:7,11; 73:23; Is 41:10; 43:2,5; Jer 30:11; Ezek 34:30; Amos 5:14; Hag 1:13; Matt 28:20; 2Cor 13:11; 2Thes 3:16; Rev 21:3
[16] Josh 1:9 NASB
[17] Jer 30:11 NASB
[18] Matt 28:20 NASB
[19] 2Cor 13:4 NASB; cf. 1Thes 5:10
[20] 2Cor 13:4 NASB

He is your God: You know that the Lord is your God.[21] You know the Father[22] and you know the Lord Jesus,[23] who is from the beginning.[24] The Lord is your portion in the land of the living.[25]

In His presence and on His mind: The Lord your God,[26] the King[27] with His kingdom,[28] is the Mighty One that saves you.[29] The Lord has taken hold of your right hand,[30] and His hand is known to you.[31] The Lord remembers you[32] and visits you every morning.[33] He keeps count of your tossings and put your tears in His bottle, recording all this in His book.[34]

... Be strong and courageous! Do not tremble or be dismayed, for the Lord your God is with you wherever you go."
Joshua 1:9 NASB

---

[21] Ex 6:7 NASB; cf. Ex 29:46; Jer 31:34; Ezek 6:7; Gal 4:9

[22] 1John 2:13 NASB; cf. 1John 5:20; Heb 8:11

[23] John 10:14 NASB; cf. Phil 3:10; 1John 2:13,14

[24] 1John 2:13,14 NKJV

[25] Ps 142:5 NKJV

[26] Zeph 3:17 NASB

[27] Zeph 3:15 NASB

[28] Luke 17:21 NASB

[29] Zeph 3:17 NKJV; cf. Jer 30:11

[30] Ps 73:23 NASB; cf. Is 41:13

[31] Is 66:14 NKJV

[32] Ps 115:12 NIV

[33] Job 7:18 ESV

[34] Ps 56:8 ESV

26. Drawn Near

Much like gravity keeps you securely on earth, so sin exerts a powerful draw on you. On a low-humidity day, try placing a tiny tissue scrap on a table. Run a comb through your hair and hold it just above the tissue. The tissue jumps to the comb above, because the force of electricity from a couple of extra electrons completely overpowers the force of gravity from the entire earth below. In effect, the law of static electricity has set the tissue free from the law of gravity. Paul uses similar language when he tells you that the law of the Spirit of life in Christ Jesus has set you free from the law of sin and death.[1] God in Christ draws you to Himself, breaking sin's death grip on you. You have been brought near to God by Christ's blood, and now He comes to you, rejoices over you, and lives in you. Christ was lifted up on the cross for you, and now you are being drawn mightily to Him. Sin and death don't stand a chance!

Draws you: You have come to Jesus[2] because the Father has drawn you[3] with gentle cords,[4] with bands of love[5] and unfailing kindness.[6] As Moses lifted up the serpent in the wilderness,[7] so Jesus,[8] the Son of Man,[9] was lifted up[10] from the earth* and has drawn you to Himself.[11]

Comes to you: Jesus does not leave you as an orphan; He comes to you.[12] In Christ Jesus[13] you have a better hope.[14] You have been brought near to God by the blood of Christ.[15] God has drawn near to you,[16] and you draw near to God[17] through Christ.[18] Jesus Christ has come in to you and dines with you, and you with Him.[19]

Pleased with you: The Lord takes great delight in you[20] and rejoices over you with singing.[21] God is not ashamed to be called your God,[22]

---

[1] Rom 8:2 NASB
[2] John 6:44 NKJV
[3] John 6:44 NKJV;
    cf. Jer 31:3;
    Hos 11:4
[4] Hos 11:4 NKJV
[5] Hos 11:4 NKJV;
    cf. Jer 31:3
[6] Jer 31:3 NIV
[7] John 3:14 NKJV;
    cf. Num 21:8-9
[8] John 12:32 NKJV
[9] John 3:14 NKJV;
    cf. John 8:28
[10] John 3:14 NKJV;
    cf. John 8:28;
    12:32
[11] John 12:32 NKJV
[12] John 14:18 NKJV
[13] Eph 2:13 NASB
[14] Heb 7:19 NASB
[15] Eph 2:13 NASB
[16] Jas 4:8 NKJV;
    cf. Ps 34:18
[17] Heb 7:19 NKJV;
    cf. Heb 7:25
[18] Heb 7:25 NKJV
[19] Rev 3:20 NKJV
[20] Zeph 3:17 NIV;
    cf. Ps 147:11;
    149:4
[21] Zeph 3:17 NIV
[22] Heb 11:16 NIV

and Jesus is not ashamed to call you His brother or sister.[23] God, your Savior, will present you blameless before His glorious presence with great joy, through Jesus Christ your Lord.[24]

Dwells in you: The Lord Almighty dwells in the high and holy place,[25] and He also dwells with you[26] and walks with you.[27] The eternal Lord God is your dwelling place.[28] Jesus and His Father have made their home with you.[29] Christ dwells in your heart through faith,[30] so where Jesus is, there you are also.[31] You have overcome the spirit of the Antichrist, because He who is in you is greater than he who is in the world.[32]

"...I have drawn you with lovingkindness."
Jeremiah 31:3 NASB

[23] Heb 2:11 NASB
[24] Jude 1:24-25 NIV
[25] Is 57:15 NKJV
[26] Is 57:15 NASB; cf. Ex 29:45-46; Lev 26:11; Num 35:34; Zech 2:10,11; 2Cor 6:16
[27] Lev 26:12 NKJV; cf. 2Cor 6:16
[28] Deut 33:27 ESV; cf. Ps 90:1
[29] John 14:23 NKJV
[30] Eph 3:17 NKJV
[31] John 12:26 NKJV
[32] 1John 4:4 NKJV

* *I.e.,* on the cross.

27. Greatly Favored

> You may know someone that was deeply hurt when a spouse or friend suddenly announced he or she had lost interest in the relationship and wanted out. Maybe this has happened you. But rest assured that your faithful God will *never* reject you or leave you. Day after day, His friendship, favor, goodness, and mercies to you are never ending. *No exceptions!*

God's friend: God is for you.[1] The Lord your God has multiplied His wondrous deeds and His thoughts toward you,[2] and His eyes are on you.[3] The friendship of the Lord is for you,[4] and His favor is for your lifetime.[5] Jesus has called you His friend.[6]

The goodness of the Lord: The Lord is good to you.[7] He rejoices in doing all the good that He promises you with all His heart and soul,[8] and He will never stop doing good to you.[9] The Lord's goodness shall surely follow you all the days of your life.[10]

His unending mercy: The rich[11] mercy of the Lord[12] crowns you,[13] and you receive mercy and find grace.[14] The Lord's mercies to you never come to an end; they are new every morning.[15]

His faithfulness: The Lord is your steadfast love,[16] and He continues His faithfulness to you.[17] The Lord delights[18] in showing faithfulness toward you.[19] All His paths are steadfast love and faithfulness for you.[20] The abundance of the Lord's steadfast love[21] crowns[22] and surrounds you.[23] The Lord directs your heart into the love of God and into

[1] Rom 8:31 NASB
[2] Ps 40:5,17 ESV
[3] 1Pet 3:12 NKJV
[4] Ps 25:14 ESV
[5] Ps 30:5 NASB
[6] John 15:15 NASB
[7] Ps 145:9 NASB; cf. Ps 23:6; 31:19; 84:11; 86:5; Lam 3:25
[8] Jer 32:41-42 ESV
[9] Jer 32:40 NIV
[10] Ps 23:6 NASB
[11] Eph 2:4 NASB
[12] Ps 145:9 ESV; cf. Ps 23:6; 103:4; Luke 1:50; Eph 2:4; Heb 4:16
[13] Ps 103:4 NKJV
[14] Heb 4:16 NIV
[15] Lam 3:22-23 ESV
[16] Ps 144:2 ESV
[17] Jer 31:3 ESV; cf. 1Cor 10:13; 2Thes 3:3
[18] Micah 7:18 ESV
[19] Micah 7:20 ESV; cf. Ex 34:6
[20] Ps 25:10 ESV
[21] Ps 5:7 ESV; cf. Ps 32:10; 103:4
[22] Ps 103:4 ESV
[23] Ps 32:10 ESV

the steadfastness of Christ,[24] who remains faithful to you.[25] Great is the Lord's faithfulness to you![26]

... [the Lord's] favor is
for a lifetime ...
Psalm 30:5 NASB

---

[24] 2Thes 3:5 NASB
[25] 2Tim 2:13 NASB

[26] Lam 3:23 ESV;
cf. Ps 31:5

28. Fully Assured

How can you be sure that God's promises and assurances really apply to you today? My younger daughter recently offered to provide party favors for a wedding reception. Wisely, the bride later called to check on her progress. Those who know my daughter, however, found this a little humorous, as she is very dependable and consistently completes projects with high quality. So, how well do you know God? What are your expectations of Him? Do you worry whether He is doing the absolute best for you? Do you fear that you had better look out for your own interests, just in case He lets you down? Knowing Him and His character, there is absolutely no question that He will keep every last one of His promises to you. How capable is God? He is almighty, great, and powerful. How consistent is He? He is true, everlasting, and eternal. How trustworthy is He? He is dependable, faithful, and steadfast. How good is He? He is holy, righteous, perfect, and just. How loving is He? He is caring, forgiving, patient, and kind. How close is He? He is comforting, compassionate, and in you. Any questions?

Sure promises: God has given you His very great and precious promises,[1] and He never lies.[2] God who promised is faithful,[3] so you receive what He has promised to you.[4] You are a child of promise,[5] and God does what He has promised to you.[6] The Lord keeps His oath to you.[7] He remembers His holy covenant with you[8] and the mercy He promised to show to you.[9] You have God's promises as a sure and steadfast anchor of your soul, a hope that enters into the inner place behind the curtain*.[10] For you, all the promises of God find their Yes in Christ.[11]

Confidence before God: The Lord is your trust and the one upon whom you lean.[12] He is your confidence[13] and hope.[14] You abound in hope by the power of the Holy Spirit,[15] and hope does not disappoint.[16]

---

[1] 2Pet 1:4 NIV
[2] Tit 1:2 ESV
[3] Heb 10:23 NIV;
  cf. Heb 11:11
[4] Heb 10:36 NIV
[5] Gal 4:28 NKJV

[6] Gen 28:15 NASB
[7] Deut 7:8 ESV
[8] Luke 1:72 NKJV;
  cf. Deut 4:31
[9] Luke 1:72 ESV
[10] Heb 6:17,19 ESV

[11] 2Cor 1:20 ESV
[12] Ps 71:5-6 ESV
[13] Prov 3:26 NKJV
[14] Jer 14:8 NKJV
[15] Rom 15:13 NKJV
[16] Rom 5:5 NKJV

The God of all grace Himself confirms[17] and establishes you[18] in Christ,[19] so that your heart does not condemn you and you have confidence before God.[20] You will serve the Lord without fear all your days.[21]

Never abandoned: The Lord God will not forget you[22] nor hide His face from you.[23] In God's great mercy He does not put an end to you[24] or abandon you,[25] for the Lord is a gracious and merciful God.[26] God will not leave you[27] or forsake you[28] for His great name's sake, because it has pleased the Lord to make you one of His people,[29] part of "A City Not Forsaken."[30] The Lord will not abandon your heritage.[31] He will not leave you in the wicked's hand or let you be condemned when you are judged.[32] You have come to Jesus, and He will never cast you out.[33]

... [God] who promised is faithful.
Hebrews 10:23 NIV

---

[17] 1Pet 5:10 NASB
[18] 1Pet 5:10 NASB; cf. 2Cor 1:21; 2Thes 3:3
[19] 2Cor 1:21 NASB; cf. 1Pet 5:10
[20] 1John 3:21 NASB; cf. Heb 10:22
[21] Luke 1:74-75 NASB
[22] Is 49:15 NASB
[23] Ezek 39:29 NASB
[24] Neh 9:31 NIV
[25] Ps 37:33 ESV; Neh 9:31 NIV
[26] Neh 9:31 NIV
[27] Deut 4:31 ESV; cf. Gen 28:15; Deut 31:6,8; Josh 1:5
[28] Ps 37:28 ESV; cf. Deut 31:6,8; Josh 1:5; 1Sam 12:22; Neh 9:31; Ps 94:14; Is 41:17
[29] 1Sam 12:22 ESV
[30] Is 62:12 NKJV
[31] Ps 94:14 ESV
[32] Ps 37:33 NASB
[33] John 6:37 ESV

* See *curtain* in glossary.

29. Deeply Comforted

During a loud thunderstorm in an unfamiliar place, a young child can become quite anxious and fearful. But in the reassuring arms of a parent, that same child can settle down, become peaceful, and even fall asleep. When Jesus found Himself weary and expended, He would head out to a remote place and spend time alone with His Father. God extends that same privilege to you. He knows how to set your heart at rest and to replace your fear and anxiety with His peace.

Cared for: The Lord of hosts cares for you,[1] and with everlasting love[2] He has compassion on you.[3] You are enabled to cast your anxieties on God, because He cares for you.[4]

Consoled: The God and Father of our Lord Jesus Christ, the Father of compassion and the God of all comfort, comforts you in all your troubles.[5] The Lord delivers your eyes from tears.[6] Your Lord Jesus Christ Himself and God your Father comfort your heart.[7] When the cares of your heart are many, the Lord's consolations cheer your soul.[8] The Lord God will quiet you with His love.[9] Jesus is gentle with you and humble of heart, so that you find rest for your soul.[10]

At peace: God the Lord speaks peace to you,[11] and He has made peace with you.[12] Jesus Himself gives His peace to you.[13] He does not give to you as the world gives.[14] The Lord of peace Himself gives you peace at all times and in every way.[15] He establishes great peace for you[16] and keeps you in perfect peace as your mind is stayed on Him.[17] The God of hope fills you with all peace in believing.[18] And the peace of God, which transcends all understanding, guards your heart and your mind in Christ Jesus.[19]

[1] Zech 10:3 ESV; cf. Deut 32:10
[2] Is 54:8 ESV
[3] Is 54:8 ESV; cf. Ex 22:27
[4] 1Pet 5:7 ESV
[5] 2Cor 1:3-4 NIV
[6] Ps 116:8 NIV
[7] 2Thes 2:16-17 NASB
[8] Ps 94:19 ESV
[9] Zeph 3:17 NKJV
[10] Matt 11:29 NASB
[11] Ps 85:8 NKJV
[12] Is 27:5 NKJV
[13] John 14:27; Luke 24:36 ESV
[14] John 14:27 NIV
[15] 2Thes 3:16 NIV
[16] Is 26:12; 54:13 NKJV
[17] Is 26:3 NKJV
[18] Rom 15:13 NKJV
[19] Phil 4:7 NIV

*Praise be to the God and Father
of our Lord Jesus Christ,
the Father of compassion
and the God of all comfort,
who comforts us in all our troubles...*
2 Corinthians 1:3-4 NIV

He Reveals Himself to You

My wife and I have now been married for over four decades. As you might guess, we have come to know each other pretty well, but it's remarkable that we continue to learn new things about each other and ourselves. How well do you know God? Praise God for all that you already have learned, but you can also be excited about all you will continue to learn. Know for sure He is deeply invested, through His Word and His Spirit, in enabling you to know Him more and more.

30. In God's Light

On one road trip my family stopped to take a ride-through cave tour. Deep inside, our guide warned us she was about to extinguish all lights for a short time. I had never experienced such absolute darkness! I wasn't at all sure that I could have ever safely found my way out of that cave without some light source. God compares life without faith in Him to walking in darkness. Through the light of God's Word, you have experienced and come to know Him who is Light. Only through Christ are you able to plainly see the truth about the darkness of your sin and the brilliance of His grace and glory. You are truly a child of Light.

Walking in the light: You have seen a great light.[1] The Lord is God, and He has made His light shine on you.[2] He calls you out of darkness into His marvelous light.[3] The Lord God is your lamp.[4] He shines in your heart[5] and lightens your darkness.[6] The Lord brings you out to the light[7] as He Himself is your light.[8] In God's light you see light,[9] and God has shone in your heart to give you the light of the knowledge of the glory of God in the face of Jesus Christ.[10] Christ came as the Light of the world,[11] and He gives light to you.[12] You follow Him[13] and

---

[1] Is 9:2 NIV
[2] Ps 118:27 NIV;
   cf. Is 9:2
[3] 1Pet 2:9 NASB
[4] 2Sam 22:29 ESV
[5] 2Cor 4:6 NASB

[6] 2Sam 22:29 ESV
[7] Micah 7:9 NASB
[8] Ps 27:1 NASB;
   cf. Micah 7:8
[9] Ps 36:9 NKJV
[10] 2Cor 4:6 NKJV

[11] John 12:46; 8:12
   ESV
[12] Luke 1:79 NKJV
[13] John 8:12 NKJV

do not walk in darkness,[14] but have the light of life.[15] You are a child of Light.[16]

God's abiding truth: You know God's truth,[17] which lives in you and will be with you forever.[18] It was His desire that you come to the knowledge of the truth.[19] The Spirit of truth guides you into all the truth,[20] for the Spirit searches everything, even the depths of God. God reveals these things to you through the Spirit.[21]

*For with You is
the fountain of life;
In Your light we see light.
Psalm 36:9 NKJV*

---

[14] John 8:12 NASB; cf. Ps 18:28; Micah 7:8; Luke 1:79; John 12:46
[15] John 8:12 NASB; cf. Ps 18:28
[16] Eph 5:8 NASB; cf. 1Thes 5:5
[17] John 8:32; 1John 2:21 NASB
[18] 2John 1:2 NIV
[19] 1Tim 2:4 NKJV
[20] John 16:13 NASB
[21] 1Cor 2:10 ESV

31. God's Effective Word

You can learn a lot about God by considering the majesty and complexity of creation. You can also understand quite a bit about His Law, since that Law is written on your own heart. But there is only one place where you can accurately learn about His love and grace for you and about His plan for your life—in His amazing Love Letter, the Bible. It isn't a book about perfect people, but about ordinary people like you in the hands of an extraordinary God. The Bible was inspired and written by God's Holy Spirit, and the Spirit is the One who enables you to understand it, believe it, and incorporate it into your life. As you read and meditate on God's Word, you become a dynamic part of His story. God's Word is truly alive and active in you!

God's Word nearby: God's Word is very near you.[1] It is in your mouth[2] and in your heart, so that you can do it.[3] The Lord teaches you out of His Word*,[4] which enlightens your eyes.[5] God's Word is a lamp to your feet and a light to your path.[6] He lights your lamp[7] and lightens your darkness.[8]

God's Word at work: God's Word is alive and active in you.[9] The Lord's testimonies are your delight and your counselors.[10] You have heard[11] and received[12] the Word,[13] and are holding it fast in an honest and good heart[14] with the joy of the Holy Spirit.[15] God's Word gives joy to your heart.[16] The Word of God lives in you[17] and is at work in you.[18]

Christ in the Word: Through the Holy Scriptures you have been made wise for salvation through faith in Christ Jesus.[19] These Scriptures testify about Him,[20] who brought life and immortality to light for you

---

[1] Deut 30:14 NASB
[2] Deut 30:14 NASB; cf. Is 51:16
[3] Deut 30:14 ESV
[4] Ps 94:12 NASB
[5] Ps 19:8 NASB
[6] Ps 119:105 NASB
[7] Ps 18:28 NASB
[8] Ps 18:28 ESV
[9] Heb 4:12 NIV
[10] Ps 119:24 NASB
[11] Luke 8:15 NASB
[12] 1Thes 1:6 NASB
[13] Luke 8:15; 1Thes 1:6 NASB
[14] Luke 8:15 ESV
[15] 1Thes 1:6 NASB
[16] Ps 19:8 NIV
[17] 1John 2:14 NIV
[18] 1Thes 2:13 ESV
[19] 2Tim 3:15 NIV
[20] John 5:39 NIV

through the gospel.[21] You live[22] and walk[23] by faith,[24] not by sight.[25] You abide in Christ's Word and are truly His disciple.[26]

And we also thank God constantly for this, that...you received the Word of God....which is at work in you believers.

1 Thessalonians 2:13 ESV

---

[21] 2Tim 1:10 NASB
[22] Heb 10:38 NASB
[23] 2Cor 5:7 NASB

[24] 2Cor 5:7;
    Heb 10:38 NASB
[25] 2Cor 5:7 NASB

[26] John 8:31 ESV

* *Literally*, law.

32. God Is Your Teacher

Some professions emphasize the importance of establishing a personal board of directors—a group of smart and experienced people who can help you avoid pitfalls and make informed decisions. How much greater value comes from consulting your wise and all-knowing God! You can think of the Father, Son, and Holy Spirit as your personal mentoring team, guiding you through the Scriptures and life. The Father gives you abundant wisdom and insight. Jesus makes the Father and Himself known to you, and establishes in you His very own mind. The Holy Spirit enables you to receive all God has for you and to never forget Him. I pray that this book may help you more fully access and apply all that God offers you.

Taught by the Father: God opens your ears [1] and instructs you properly, [2] and great is your peace. [3] He teaches you [4] and makes His covenant known to you. [5] The Lord gives you sound wisdom, [6] knowledge, [7] and understanding [8] in abundance, [9] generously and without reproach. [10] God teaches you wisdom in the secret heart, [11] and to you it has been granted to know the mysteries of the kingdom of heaven. [12] You have sought and found God, [13] and He rewards you. [14] You have knocked, and to you it has been opened. [15] Your eyes see and your ears hear. [16]

Taught by the Son: Words of the wise are given to you by one Shepherd. [17] The Son, [18] the Wisdom of God, [19] has chosen to reveal the Father [20] and to disclose Himself to you. [21] All that Jesus heard from His Father, He has made known to you. [22] You comprehend what is the breadth and length and height and depth, and know the love of

---

[1] Ps 40:6 NASB
[2] Is 28:26 NASB
[3] Is 54:13 NKJV
[4] Is 28:26 NKJV; cf. Is 54:13
[5] Ps 25:14 NIV
[6] Prov 2:6-7 NASB; cf. Eccl 2:26; Is 33:6; Eph 1:8; James 1:5
[7] Prov 2:6 NASB; cf. Eccl 2:26; Is 33:6
[8] Prov 2:6 NASB; cf. Eph 1:8
[9] Is 33:6 ESV
[10] Jas 1:5 NASB
[11] Ps 51:6 ESV
[12] Matt 13:11 NASB; cf. Eph 1:8
[13] Jer 29:13-14 NASB;
cf. Matt 7:7-8; Luke 11:9-10
[14] Heb 11:6 NASB
[15] Matt 7:7-8; Luke 11:9-10 NASB
[16] Matt 13:16 NASB
[17] Eccl 12:11 NASB
[18] Luke 10:22 NIV
[19] 1Cor 1:24 NIV
[20] Luke 10:22 NIV
[21] John 14:21 NASB
[22] John 15:15 NKJV

Christ which surpasses knowledge.[23] You know that the Son of God has come, and has given you understanding so that you know Him who is true.[24] You have the mind of Christ.[25]

Taught by the Spirit: You have received the Spirit who is from God, that you may know the things freely given to you by God.[26] The Holy Spirit, whom the Father has sent to you in Jesus' name, will teach you all things and will remind you of everything Jesus has said to you.[27] He takes what is Jesus' and declares it to you.[28] The anointing that you received from the Holy One abides in you,[29] and you have knowledge.[30] You have no need that anyone should teach you, as His anointing teaches you about everything, and is true.[31] You judge all things, but are yourself to be judged by no one.[32]

All your children will be taught by the Lord, and great will be their peace.

Isaiah 54:13 NIV

---

[23] Eph 3:18-19 NASB
[24] 1John 5:20 NASB
[25] 1Cor 2:16 NASB
[26] 1Cor 2:12 NASB
[27] John 14:26 NIV
[28] John 16:13-15 NKJV
[29] 1John 2:20,27 NKJV
[30] 1John 2:20 ESV
[31] 1John 2:27 ESV
[32] 1Cor 2:15 ESV

33. Talking with God

Have you ever watched a sit-com routine, in which two people are discussing something about a third person that is standing nearby, as if he or she wasn't there? That person may interject with irritation, "You know, I'm right here and I can hear you." How often God must feel that way as we talk about Him almost as if He wasn't really present and listening! What enables your faith to be more than a set of doctrines and principles, or a mere history lesson, is your interaction with the God to whom your faith points. You hear what He has to tell you. You talk to Him in prayer and in expectation, as a young child might with a parent. God doesn't only want you to talk *about* Him but also *with* Him. Perhaps God is saying right now, "You know, I'm right here and I can hear you."

You know Jesus' voice: You hear Jesus' voice,[1] that of your Good Shepherd,[2] and have opened the door.[3] Your eyes see your Teacher, and your ears hear a word behind you, saying, "This is the way, walk in it," when you turn to the right or when you turn to the left.[4]

God hears when you call: Through Jesus Christ your Lord, you have[5] boldness[6] and confident access[7] in one Spirit[8] to the Father.[9] The Lord is so near to you;[10] He pays attention to you[11] and hears you[12] from heaven[13] when you pray to Him.[14] While you are still speaking, the Lord hears.[15] The Lord's ears are attentive to your prayer.[16] When you call or cry out to the Lord,[17] He hears[18] and says, "Here I am,"[19] and He saves you,[20] for the Lord is compassionate.[21]

---

[1] John 10:27 NASB; cf. Rev 3:20
[2] John 10:14 NASB
[3] Rev 3:20 NASB
[4] Is 30:20-21 ESV
[5] Eph 2:18 NASB; cf. Eph 3:12
[6] Eph 3:12 NASB
[7] Eph 3:12 NASB; cf. Eph 2:18
[8] Eph 2:18 NASB
[9] Eph 2:18 NASB; cf. Eph 3:12
[10] Deut 4:7 NKJV; cf. Ps 145:18
[11] Mal 3:16 ESV
[12] Ps 4:3 NASB; cf. 2Chron 7:14; Prov 15:29; Jer 29:12; Micah 7:7; Mal 3:16
[13] 2Chron 7:14 NASB
[14] Jer 29:12 ESV
[15] Is 65:24 NIV
[16] 1Pet 3:12 NIV; cf. Ps 34:15
[17] Ps 4:3; Ex 22:27 NIV; cf. Deut 4:7; Ps 34:17; 145:19; Is 58:9
[18] Ps 34:17 NASB; cf. Ex 22:27; Ps 145:19
[19] Is 58:9 NASB
[20] Ps 145:19 NASB
[21] Ex 22:27 NIV

God answers your prayer: God gives you good things when you ask Him.[22] This is the confidence you have in approaching God: that if you ask anything according to His will, He hears you.[23] The Lord answers you[24] when you call to Him,[25] and even before you call,[26] and you have the requests that you have asked of Him.[27] As you do what pleases God,[28] whatever you ask in prayer[29] in Jesus' name,[30] believing that you have received it,[31] it will be yours.[32] If you say to a mountain, "Be taken up and thrown into the sea," and do not doubt in your heart, but believe that what you say will come to pass, it will be done for you.[33] Your prayer is powerful and effective.[34]

The Spirit helps you: The Spirit also helps your weakness; for you do not know how to pray as you should, but the Spirit Himself intercedes for you with groanings too deep for words; and God who searches the heart knows what the mind of the Spirit is, because the Spirit intercedes for you according to the will of God.[35]

Before they call I will answer;
while they are still speaking I will hear.
Isaiah 65:24 NIV

---

[22] Matt 7:11 NKJV
[23] 1John 5:14 NIV
[24] Ps 91:15 NIV;
cf. Is 41:17; 58:9;
65:24
[25] Ps 91:15 ESV;
cf. Is 58:9
[26] Is 65:24 NASB
[27] 1John 5:15 ESV
[28] 1John 3:22 NIV

[29] Matt 21:22; Mark
11:24 ESV;
cf. Matt 7:7-8;
Luke 11:9-10;
John 15:7;
1John 3:22
[30] John 14:13 NIV
[31] Mark 11:24 NIV;
cf. Matt 21:22

[32] Mark 11:24 NIV;
cf. Matt 7:7-8;
21:22; Luke 11:9-
10; John 14:13;
15:7; 1John 3:22
[33] Mark 11:23 ESV;
cf. John 15:7
[34] Jas 5:16 NIV
[35] Rom 8:26-27
NASB

34. Receiving His Counsel

Let's skip the clichéd jokes about men never asking for directions, and admit that in our faith life we all often go it alone. More disturbing than failing to ask directions is failing to know where you are going in the first place. God offers you full concierge service. He continually guides and advises you in your daily choices and decisions. In His unfailing love, He leads you in righteousness throughout your life's journey. He shepherds you and ensures that you are fed spiritually. He also directs you to walk obediently and to choose your way wisely. You've got the smartest Guy in the world living inside you—*the* Counselor. Do you suppose it might be worth consulting with Him?

Guided: You receive direction from the Lord,[1] and He guides you with His counsel.[2] You do not live on bread alone, but on every word that comes from the mouth of God.[3] For His name's sake[4] the Lord guides you[5] continually[6] and forever.[7] Jesus Christ guides your feet into the way of peace.[8] The Lord gives His good Spirit,[9] the Counselor,[10] to instruct you[11] and lead you.[12]

Led: In His unfailing love,[13] the Lord leads you[14] in what is right[15] with cords of kindness and the bands of love.[16] He leads you[17] in paths of righteousness[18] for His name's sake.[19] The Lord will guard your going out and your coming in from this time forth and forever.[20] If you take the wings of the dawn, if you dwell in the remotest part of the sea, even there His hand will lead you.[21]

[1] Deut 33:3 ESV; cf. Ps 25:9
[2] Ps 73:24 NIV; cf. Ps 16:7
[3] Matt 4:4 NIV
[4] Ps 31:3 NASB
[5] Ps 31:3 NASB; cf. Ps 48:14; Is 58:11; Luke 1:79
[6] Is 58:11 NASB
[7] Ps 48:14 ESV
[8] Luke 1:79 NASB
[9] Neh 9:20 NIV
[10] John 14:16 RSV
[11] Neh 9:20 NIV
[12] Gal 5:18 NIV
[13] Ex 15:13 NIV
[14] Ex 15:13 NIV; cf. Ps 139:10; Hos 11:4
[15] Ps 25:9 ESV
[16] Hos 11:4 ESV
[17] Ps 31:3 NASB; cf. Ps 23:3; 25:9
[18] Ps 23:3 ESV
[19] Ps 23:3 NASB; cf. Ps 31:3
[20] Ps 121:8 NASB
[21] Ps 139:9-10 NASB

Overseen: The Lord God is your Shepherd,[22] and you are a sheep of His pasture.[23] He set up over you one Shepherd,[24] Christ, who rules and[25] shepherds you.[26] You were straying like a sheep but have now returned to the Shepherd and Overseer of your soul.[27] The Lord gives you shepherds[28] after His own heart,[29] who care for you.[30] God sent these to preach to you, leading you to believe in Him[31] and feeding you with knowledge and understanding.[32]

Directed: The Lord makes your paths straight[33] and level.[34] He makes known to you the path of life[35] and instructs you in the way[36] that you should choose.[37] The Lord has put His Spirit within you and causes you to walk in His statutes and to be careful to obey His rules.[38] He makes your way blameless[39] and guides you by His strength to His holy abode.[40]

Trust in the Lord with all your heart,
And lean not on your own understanding;
In all your ways acknowledge Him,
And He shall direct your paths.
Proverbs 3:5-6 NKJV

---

[22] Ps 23:1 NASB; *cf.* Ps 80:1; Ezek 34:23; Matt 2:6; 1Pet 2:25
[23] Ps 79:13; 100:3 NASB
[24] Ezek 34:23 NASB; *cf.* Ezek 37:24
[25] Matt 2:6 NASB
[26] Matt 2:6 NASB; *cf.* Ezek 34:23
[27] 1Pet 2:25 ESV
[28] Jer 3:15 NASB; *cf.* Jer 23:4
[29] Jer 3:15 NASB
[30] Jer 23:4 ESV
[31] Rom 10:14-15 NIV
[32] Jer 3:15 ESV
[33] Prov 3:6 NIV
[34] Is 26:7 NIV
[35] Ps 16:11; Acts 2:28 NIV
[36] Ps 25:8,12 NASB
[37] Ps 25:12 NASB
[38] Ezek 36:27 ESV
[39] 2Sam 22:33 ESV
[40] Ex 15:13 ESV

Today

He Comes to Your Aid

Who was your favorite superhero growing up? Mine was Superman, but you may have gravitated toward another. The mighty and good hero stands up against overwhelming odds to protect ordinary citizens from danger and evil. In that sense, superheroes are types of Christ. Christ prevailed at great cost in the epic battle between God's kingdom of light and the devil's kingdom of darkness. In Christ you are never alone and always kept safe. The Lord is actively involved in your life and committed to protecting you. You can rest assured that He's "got your back"—and every other part of you, for that matter!

35. Your Shepherd

> If you were asked to design a mentoring program for a future king, what might it include? How about a multi-year assignment caring for helpless sheep in a little suburb of Jerusalem? No, that wouldn't have crossed my mind either, but it is the exact training that God provided for His future king, David! David's early years of protecting and caring for sheep taught him how later to care for his subjects. His beautiful and beloved Psalm 23 reflects how God is your Shepherd, and how as a result you have everything that you need. Your Shepherd tends to your needs, protects you from danger and predators, and guards you with His life. You learn to trust your Shepherd, even in scary times, and He comforts you and eases your fears. It's good to be one of His sheep!

Kept: The Lord God tends His flock, including you, like a shepherd.[1] He is your Keeper,[2] who keeps you as a shepherd keeps his flock.[3] Wherever you go[4] He keeps you[5] night and day,[6] and He neither slumbers nor sleeps.[7] The eyes of the Lord[8] are in every place,[9] keeping watch on you[10] and your way.[11]

---

[1] Is 40:11 NIV
[2] Ps 121:5; Is 27:3 NASB
[3] Jer 31:10 NASB; *cf.* Is 40:11
[4] Gen 28:15 NASB

[5] Is 42:6 ESV; *cf.* Gen 28:15; Num 6:24; Ps 12:7; 121:3-4,7-8; Is 27:3
[6] Is 27:3 NKJV
[7] Ps 121:3-4 NKJV

[8] Prov 15:3 NKJV; *cf.* Ps 33:18
[9] Prov 15:3 NKJV
[10] Prov 15:3 NKJV; *cf.* Ps 33:18; Prov 2:8; Jer 12:3
[11] Prov 2:8 ESV

Carried: The Lord bears you up[12] and carries you.[13] Like a shepherd, He gathers you in His arms and carries you close to his heart.[14] You have been borne by the Lord from before your birth and carried from the womb.[15] Even to your graying years and old age He will be the same and will bear you.[16] No one can snatch you out of Jesus' hand or His Father's hand.[17]

Protected: The Lord of hosts protects you,[18] and you have laid hold of His protection.[19] As your Shepherd, the Lord anoints your head with oil*.[20] Christ who was born of God protects you, and the evil one does not touch you.[21]

Safe: The Lord makes you dwell in safety.[22] Even though you walk in the midst of trouble,[23] through the valley of the shadow of death, you fear no evil,[24] for the Lord is with you;[25] His rod and His staff, they comfort you.[26] It is the Lord that redeems[27] and keeps[28] your life,[29] though a thousand may fall at your side or ten thousand at your right hand.[30]

He tends His flock like a shepherd;
He gathers the lambs in His arms and
carries them close to His heart...
Isaiah 40:11 NIV

[12] Ps 68:19 ESV; *cf.* Is 46:4; 63:9
[13] Is 46:4 NKJV; *cf.* Is 63:9
[14] Is 40:11 NIV
[15] Is 46:3 ESV
[16] Is 46:4 NASB
[17] John 10:28-29 NIV
[18] Zech 9:15 ESV; *cf.* Ps 41:2; 91:14
[19] Is 27:5 ESV
[20] Ps 23:1,5 NASB
[21] 1John 5:18 ESV
[22] Ps 4:8 NASB
[23] Ps 138:7 NASB
[24] Ps 23:4 NASB; *cf.* Is 43:2
[25] Ps 23:4 NASB; *cf.* Gen 28:15; Deut 31:8; Josh 1:9; Ps 14:5; 46:7,11; 73:23; Is 41:10; 43:5; Zeph 3:15
[26] Ps 23:4 NASB
[27] Lam 3:58 NIV
[28] Ps 121:7 NIV
[29] Ps 121:7 NIV; *cf.* Ps 138:7; Lam 3:58
[30] Ps 91:7 NIV

* See *anointed* in glossary.

36. Your Savior

> When facing grave danger from foes, you need a Savior. When ancient Israel turned to God, He would raise up judges or saviors to route their enemies and to restore peace. What an incredible Savior you now have in your Lord Jesus Christ! He saves you from the power of evil and from God's wrath over sin. The Lord is indeed mighty to save you!

He saves you: The Lord God alone[1] is the God of your salvation.[2] He Himself is your Savior[3] and Helper;[4] your salvation[5] and a very present help[6] in time of trouble.[7] God most high[8] comes[9] and saves you[10] from violence[11] and from foes.[12] The angel of the Lord's presence saves you.[13] You look to the Lord and wait for Him.[14] His salvation is near to you,[15] and your salvation rests on Him.[16] The Lord is the stability of your times and a wealth of salvation.[17]

You are helped: Your help comes from the Lord, who made heaven and earth.[18] The Lord God rides across the heavens[19] to help you.[20] He sends from on high and takes you; He draws you out of many waters.[21] The Lord goes out for your salvation.[22] He sends out His angels as ministering spirits to render service for your sake.[23]

[1] Ps 62:2,6 ESV
[2] Ps 25:5; 51:14; 79:9; Hab 3:18 NASB; cf. Ps 62:1; Is 17:10; Hab 3:13
[3] 2Sam 22:3 NASB; cf. Is 43:11; Jer 14:8
[4] Heb 13:6; Ps 54:4; NASB; cf. Ps 28:7; 33:20; 37:40; 40:17; 63:7; 70:5; Is 41:10,14; 44:2
[5] Ex 15:2; Ps 62:2,6; 118:14 NASB;
cf. Ps 38:22
[6] Ps 46:1 NASB
[7] Jer 14:8 ESV; cf. Ps 46:1; 91:15
[8] Ps 57:2 NKJV
[9] Is 35:4 NKJV; cf. Ps 57:3; Is 62:11
[10] Is 35:4 NKJV; cf. Deut 33:29; 2Sam 22:3,18; Ps 7:10; 37:40; 44:7; 57:3; 145:19; Is 46:4; 62:11; Zeph 3:17; Zech 8:13
[11] 2Sam 22:3 NKJV
[12] Ps 44:7 ESV; cf. 2Sam 22:18
[13] Is 63:9 NKJV
[14] Micah 7:7 NKJV
[15] Ps 85:9 NASB
[16] Ps 62:7 ESV
[17] Is 33:6 NASB
[18] Ps 121:2 NASB; cf. Ps 124:8
[19] Deut 33:26 NIV
[20] Deut 33:26 NIV; cf. Heb 2:16; 4:16
[21] 2Sam 22:17 NASB
[22] Hab 3:13 ESV
[23] Heb 1:14 NASB

Working on your behalf: The Lord is on your side as your helper.[24] He takes up[25] your case[26] and is working for you.[27] Jesus Christ appears for you in God's presence[28] and always lives to intercede for you.[29]

"I, even I, am the Lord,
And there is no Savior besides Me."
Isaiah 43:11 NASB

---

[24] Ps 118:7 ESV
[25] Lam 3:58 NIV
[26] Lam 3:58 NIV;
  cf. Micah 7:9

[27] Ps 31:19 ESV
[28] Heb 9:24 NIV

[29] Heb 7:25 NIV;
  cf. Is 53:12;
  Rom 8:34

37. Your Deliverer

So much is broken in our fallen world. We can fall prey to sorrow, disappointments, losses, broken appliances, accidents, injuries, illnesses, cancers, or damage from fire, water, wind, or hail. But none of these can ever cause a rift between you and your God. He knows exactly how to deliver and rescue you. He knows which trials will make you stronger and which must be resolved, which struggles will make you a greater blessing to others and which would not. In all this He wants you to know that He delights in rescuing you and works all for your good.

He rescues you: The Lord is your Deliverer[1] and Rescuer. He rescues you,[2] because he delights in you.[3] The angel of the Lord delivers you.[4] Many are your afflictions[5] and trials,[6] and the Lord knows how[7] to rescue[8] and deliver you[9] out of all them all.[10] You are not afraid of the terror by night or of the destruction that lays waste at noon.[11] The Lord draws you up from the pit of destruction, out of the miry bog,[12] and He redeems your life from the pit.[13] It is the Lord who keeps your foot from being caught.[14]

More than conqueror: Who shall separate you from the love of Christ? Shall distress, or famine, or nakedness, or danger?[15] No, in all these things you are more than a conqueror through Him who loved you.[16] In Christ you find grace to help you in your time of need.[17] The Lord surrounds you with songs of deliverance.[18]

[1] Ps 18:2 NASB;
cf. 2Sam 22:2;
Ps 34:17,19; 37:40;
41:1; 50:15; 70:5;
91:3,14; 97:10;
144:2
[2] Ps 91:15 NASB;
cf. 2Sam 22:20;
2Pet 2:9
[3] 2Sam 22:20 NASB
[4] Ps 34:7 NKJV
[5] Ps 34:19 NKJV
[6] 2Pet 2:9 NIV
[7] 2Pet 2:9 NIV
[8] 2Pet 2:9 NIV;
cf. 2Sam 22:20;
Ps 91:15
[9] Ps 34:17,19 NIV;
cf. Ps 37:40; 41:1;
50:15; 91:3,14;
97:10
[10] Ps 34:19 NASB;
cf. Ps 34:17;
2Pet 2:9
[11] Ps 91:5-6 NASB
[12] Ps 40:2 ESV
[13] Ps 103:4 NASB
[14] Prov 3:26 NASB
[15] Rom 8:35 ESV
[16] Rom 8:37 NIV
[17] Heb 4:16 NIV
[18] Ps 32:7 NASB

...You surround me with songs of deliverance.
Psalm 32:7 NASB

38. Your Place of Refuge

I'm supposing that one of the last places you'd choose to be left alone is on an open field with hordes of enemies rapidly approaching. You would probably search desperately for a place of protection to hide yourself. Spiritually, you find yourself on such a battlefield. But the great news is that you have found a secure fortress in your Lord. Your life is built on the Rock that cannot be moved. In the day of distress, you can remain steadfast, for your life is safely hidden in Christ.

Your Rock: The Lord God is your mighty[1] and everlasting[2] Rock,[3] the Rock of your salvation.[4] There is no unrighteousness in Him.[5] Who is a rock, except your God?[6]—the God who equips you with strength and makes your way blameless.[7] He is the Rock that is higher than you.[8] The Lord lifts you up[9] and sets your feet[10] high[11] upon a rock,[12] making your steps secure.[13] He is the Rock of your refuge.[14]

Your Fortress: The Lord God is your strong[15] and saving[16] Refuge[17] in the day of trouble[18] or distress,[19] a strong Tower against your enemy.[20] You take refuge in the Lord[21] and in the Son, and you are blessed.[22] Only the Lord[23] is your Fortress.[24] In times of trouble[25] you

---

[1] Ps 62:7 NIV
[2] Is 26:4 NASB
[3] Ps 144:1 NKJV; cf. 2Sam 22:2,32; 23:3; Ps 18:2,31,46; 28:1; 31:3; 42:9; 62:2,6, 7; 71:3; 78:35; 92:15; Is 17:10; 26:4; Hab 1:12
[4] Ps 95:1 NKJV; cf. 2Sam 22:47
[5] Ps 92:15 NKJV
[6] Ps 18:31 NKJV; cf. 2Sam 22:32; Ps 62:6
[7] Ps 18:32 ESV
[8] Ps 61:2 NASB

[9] Ps 27:5 NASB
[10] Ps 40:2 NASB
[11] Ps 27:5 NKJV
[12] Ps 27:5 NKJV; cf. Ps 40:2
[13] Ps 40:2 ESV
[14] Is 17:10 ESV; cf. 2Sam 22:2-3; Ps 18:2; 62:7
[15] Ps 71:7 ESV; cf. 2Sam 22:33
[16] 2Sam 22:3 NKJV
[17] Ps 142:5 ESV; cf. 2Sam 22:3,33; Ps 14:6; 28:8; 31:4; 46:1; 59:16; 61:3; 62:7,8; 71:7; 91:2; Is 17:10;

Jer 16:19; Joel 3:16
[18] Jer 16:19 ESV; cf. Ps 9:9; 37:39; 91:2-4
[19] Ps 59:16 NASB
[20] Ps 61:3 ESV
[21] Ps 18:2 NASB; cf. 2Sam 22:3,31; Ps 2:12; 34:8; 144:2
[22] Ps 2:12 NASB
[23] Ps 62:6 NASB
[24] Ps 59:9 NIV; cf. 2Sam 22:2; Ps 18:2; 31:3; 46:7,11; 59:16,17; 62:2,6; 71:3; 91:2
[25] Ps 59:16 NIV

take refuge in Him[26] and you are not greatly shaken.[27] The Lord[28] and His way[29] is your Stronghold,[30] the stronghold of your life.[31]

Your Hiding Place: The Lord is your Hiding Place.[32] He hides you in His shelter in the day of trouble. He conceals you under the cover of His tent,[33] where you dwell forever.[34] The Lord is a refuge from the storm and a shade from the heat for you.[35] He covers you in the shadow of His hand,[36] and you dwell beneath His shadow.[37] The Lord is your shade at your right hand; the sun does not harm you by day, nor the moon by night.[38]

Under His wings: The Lord is like an eagle that stirs up its nest and hovers over you, spreading its wings to catch you and carrying you aloft.[39] God covers you with His feathers,[40] and you take refuge[41] under the shelter[42] of His wings.[43]

*He shall cover you with His feathers,
And under His wings
you shall take refuge...*

Psalm 91:4 NKJV

---

[26] Ps 18:2 NASB
[27] Ps 62:2,6 NASB
[28] Ps 18:2 NASB;
  cf. 2Sam 22:3;
  Ps 9:9; 37:39;
  144:2; Is 25:4;
  Jer 16:19;
  Joel 3:16
[29] Prov 10:29
  NASB

[30] Ps 18:2 NASB;
  cf. 2Sam 22:3;
  Ps 9:9; 37:39;
  144:2; Prov 10:29;
  Is 25:4; Jer 16:19;
  Joel 3:16
[31] Ps 27:1 NIV
[32] Ps 32:7 NIV
[33] Ps 27:5 ESV
[34] Ps 61:4 NASB
[35] Is 25:4 NASB

[36] Is 51:16 NASB
[37] Hos 14:7 ESV;
  cf. Ps 91:1
[38] Ps 121:5-6 NIV
[39] Deut 32:11 NIV
[40] Ps 91:4 NIV
[41] Ps 61:4 NIV;
  cf. Ps 36:7; 91:4
[42] Ps 61:4 ESV
[43] Ps 61:4 NASB;
  cf. Ps 36:7; 91:4

39. Your Strength and Shield

> I remember a movie scene in which a man attempts to demon-
> strate his strength to a lady by shoving a large sofa through a
> small doorway. When she tells him that he can start pushing,
> he meekly replies, "I already did." Do you sometimes feel weak
> and inadequate as you attempt to do what God asks of you? If
> so, you are being quite realistic. Although you are weak, the
> Lord reminds you that *He* is your Strength and your Shield, and
> that *His* strength is made perfect in your weakness.

Your Strength: The Lord God, the Lord Almighty,[1] is your Strength,[2]
and He is the strength[3] and horn*[4] of your salvation.[5] The Lord is a
very present help in trouble.[6] By His favor[7] your horn is exalted[8] like
that of a wild ox.[9] You wait for the Lord and renew your strength.[10]
God is the strength of your heart.[11] The Lord makes your bones
strong,[12] and He is the glory of your strength.[13] The God of all grace
Himself[14] strengthens you[15] and makes you strong in Him,[16] in the
strength of His might.[17] The Lord is your Mighty One.[18]

Your Shield: Your shield is with God.[19] The Lord God is Himself your
Shield,[20] and the shield of your help[21] as you take refuge in Him.[22] The
Lord surrounds you with His favor as with a shield.[23] God's faithfulness to you is a shield and buckler.[24] The Lord is the Sword of your
triumph.[25] The Lord God gave you the shield of His salvation, His

---

[1] Zech 12:5 NIV
[2] Ps 59:9,17 ESV;
cf. Ex 15:2; Ps
18:1; 28:7,8; 46:1;
81:1; 118:14;
140:7; Is 28:6;
Jer 16:19; Hab
3:19; Zech 12:5
[3] Ps 140:7 NKJV
[4] Ps 18:2 NKJV;
cf. 2Sam 22:3;
Luke 1:69
[5] Ps 18:2; 140:7
NKJV; *cf.* 2Sam
22:3; Luke 1:69
[6] Ps 46:1 NKJV
[7] Ps 89:17 NASB

[8] Ps 89:17 NASB;
cf. Ps 92:10
[9] Ps 92:10 NIV
[10] Is 40:31 ESV
[11] Ps 73:26 NASB
[12] Is 58:11 ESV
[13] Ps 89:17 NASB
[14] 1Pet 5:10 NASB
[15] 1Pet 5:10 NASB;
cf. Is 40:31; 41:10
[16] Zech 10:12 ESV;
cf. 1Chron 29:12;
Eph 6:10;
1John 2:14
[17] Eph 6:10 NASB
[18] Is 49:26 NASB

[19] Ps 7:10 NASB;
cf. Ps 89:18
[20] Ps 28:7 NASB;
cf. 2Sam 22:3,31;
Ps 3:3; 18:2,30;
33:20; 59:11;
84:11; 115:9-11;
119:114; 144:2;
Prov 2:7
[21] Deut 33:29
NASB;
cf. Ps 115:9-11
[22] Prov 30:5 NASB
[23] Ps 5:12 NIV
[24] Ps 91:4 ESV
[25] Deut 33:29 ESV

right hand supports you,[26] and His gentleness makes you great.[27] He is a Sun and Shield to you,[28] and for you the sun of righteousness shall rise with healing in its wings.[29]

> *The Lord is my strength and my shield; my heart trusts in Him, and He helps me. My heart leaps for joy, and with my song I praise Him.*
> *Psalm 28:7 NIV*

[26] Ps 18:35 ESV
[27] 2Sam 22:36;
  Ps 18:35 NKJV
[28] Ps 84:11 NKJV
[29] Mal 4:2 ESV
* See *horn* in glossary.

He Enables You to Stand

Life in this world can be very challenging, to say the least. God sometimes allows extremely difficult situations to occur that you never
would have chosen. But God doesn't leave you to fend for yourself.
He remains with you on each journey through the "valley of the
shadow of death,"[1] and He miraculously works even apparent disasters
together for your good. It won't be long until these trials are gone
forever, and you can be certain that, by His grace and power, at the
end you will still be standing.

40. Rescued from Your Enemies

Ancient Israel's enemies are familiar, such as the Philistines, the
Hittites, or the Amorites. Yet the real enemy of God's people
was never truly a set of people, but the devil and his influence.
Today this is just as true as ever. You face ill will and problems
from those who are in rebellion against God. This might take
the form of full-on persecution or of a more subtle loss of position, reputation, prestige, or credibility. Yet in all this, God still
knows how to rescue you from your enemies. He protects you
on every front. Nothing can happen to you without His permission and without Him working it together for your good. He
promises that you will not be put to shame. Jesus wants you to
love and pray for your enemies, since your heavenly Father
takes no pleasure in the death of the wicked,[2] but desires that
everyone be saved.[3]

Your true enemy: Your struggle is not against flesh and blood, but
against the rulers, against the authorities, against the powers of this
dark world and against the spiritual forces of evil in the heavenly
realms.[4] The Lord guards you from the evil one.[5]

Protected from evil: Your Father in heaven[6] keeps[7] and delivers you[8]
from all evil.[9] It is God who delivers you[10] from the hand of the

---

[1] Ps 23:4 NKJV
[2] Ezek 33:11 NASB;
  cf. Ezek 18:23
[3] 1Tim 2:4
[4] Eph 6:12 NIV
[5] 2Thes 3:3 NKJV
[6] Matt 6:9 NKJV
[7] Ps 121:7 ESV
[8] Matt 6:13 NASB
[9] Ps 121:7 NASB;
  cf. Matt 6:13
[10] 2King 17:39
  NASB;
  cf. Ps 18:3; 37:40;

wicked[11] and your enemies,[12] from those who hate you,[13] for they are too strong for you.[14] He does not give you up to their will.[15] The Lord takes you out of the net that others have hidden for you[16] and will never permit you to be moved.[17]

The Lord fights alongside you: It is the Lord your God who goes with you, to fight for you against your enemies.[18] Your King is close at hand*;[19] you shall never again fear evil.[20] You believe in Jesus Christ[21] and look to your Lord,[22] who declares that you shall never be put to shame[23] in evil times.[24] You have overcome the evil one.[25]

Equipped with God's armor: The Lord provides you with His full armor, so that you will be able to stand firm against the schemes of the devil[26] and to resist in the evil day, and having done everything, to stand firm.[27] God equips you with the belt of truth; the breastplate of righteousness;[28] as shoes for your feet, the readiness given by the gospel of peace;[29] the shield of faith, with which you are able to extinguish all the flaming arrows of the evil one;[30] the helmet of salvation; and the sword of the Spirit, which is the Word of God.[31]

*"... But take heart!
I have overcome the world."
John 16:33 NIV*

97:10; Zeph 3:15;
Luke 1:71,74
[11] Ps 97:10 NASB;
cf. Ps 37:40
[12] 2King 17:39
NASB; cf. Ps
18:3; Zeph 3:15;
Luke 1:71,74
[13] 2Sam 22:18
NASB;
cf. Ps 44:7
[14] 2Sam 22:18 NASB
[15] Ps 41:2 ESV
[16] Ps 31:4 ESV

[17] Ps 55:22 NKJV
[18] Deut 20:4 NASB;
cf. Deut 31:6
[19] Zeph 3:15 NASB;
cf. Jer 14:9; Joel
2:27; Luke 17:21
[20] Zeph 3:15 ESV;
cf. Ps 23:4
[21] 1Pet 2:6 NASB
[22] Ps 34:5 NIV
[23] Joel 2:27 NKJV;
cf. Ps 25:3; 34:5;
37:19; Rom 9:33;
10:11; 1Pet 2:6

[24] Ps 37:19 ESV
[25] 1John 2:13,14
NASB
[26] Eph 6:11 NASB
[27] Eph 6:13 NASB
[28] Eph 6:14 NIV
[29] Eph 6:15 ESV
[30] Eph 6:16 NASB
[31] Eph 6:17 NASB

* *Literally,* in your midst.

41. Sharing in Christ's Suffering

Don't be surprised! Since the non-believing world treated Jesus horribly, should you as His follower expect better treatment? Jesus' disciples rejoiced to be counted worthy to suffer for His name. Jesus forewarns you that those who hate Him will hate you as well. People in rebellion against God want to avoid or silence any reminders of God's involvement and authority in their lives. So as you strive to live your life faithful to Him and His ways, you become unsettling to them. When persecution takes place, the Holy Spirit gives you words and wisdom for each situation. Be assured that restoration is coming and all persecution is only temporary. Unrepented evil will ultimately be charged against those who carry it out against you.

Forewarned of persecution: As an heir of God and co-heir with Christ,[1] you share Christ's sufferings,[2] becoming like Him in His death,[3] in order that you may also share in His glory.[4] You are blessed when people insult you and persecute you, and falsely say all kinds of evil against you because of Christ, for your reward in heaven is great.[5] You desire to live a godly life in Christ Jesus, and so you will be persecuted.[6] Your adversary, the devil, prowls around like a roaring lion, seeking someone to devour.[7] You are enabled to resist him, firm in your faith, knowing that the same kinds of suffering are being experienced by your fellow believers* throughout the world.[8]

The Spirit gives you words: Should you be arrested[9] for Christ's sake[10] and brought to trial[11] to bear witness before unbelievers**,[12] you need not worry beforehand[13] about how you should defend yourself[14] or what you should say.[15] The Holy Spirit will teach you in that very hour what you ought to say,[16] for it is not you speaking, but the Holy

---

[1] Rom 8:17 NIV
[2] Phil 3:10 ESV;
  cf. Rom 8:17
[3] Phil 3:10 NIV
[4] Rom 8:17 NIV
[5] Matt 5:11-12 NASB
[6] 2Tim 3:12 ESV
[7] 1Pet 5:8 NASB
[8] 1Pet 5:9 ESV
[9] Mark 13:11 NIV
[10] Matt 10:18 NASB
[11] Mark 13:11 NIV;
  cf. Matt 10:18;
  Luke 12:11
[12] Matt 10:18 ESV
[13] Mark 13:11 NIV,
  cf. Matt 10:19;
  Luke 12:11
[14] Luke 12:11 NIV;
  cf. Matt 10:19
[15] Luke 12:11 NKJV;
  cf. Matt 10:19;
  Mark 13:11
[16] Luke 12:12 NKJV;
  cf. Mark 13:11

Spirit.[17] Jesus will give you words and wisdom that none of your adversaries will be able to resist or contradict.[18]

Promised restoration: You know for sure[19] that neither persecution nor sword,[20] nor angels nor rulers, nor powers,[21] nor anything else in all creation, will be able to separate you from the love of God in Christ Jesus your Lord.[22] God counts you worthy of the kingdom of God, for which you are suffering.[23] After you have suffered a little while, the God of all grace, who has called you to his eternal glory in Christ, will Himself restore, confirm, strengthen, and establish you.[24] Jesus Christ gave Himself for your sins to deliver you from the present evil age, according to the will of your God and Father.[25] The Lord declares that you shall fear no more, nor be dismayed,[26] and that no one will make you afraid.[27] You can confidently say, "The Lord is my helper; I will not fear; what can man do to me?"[28]

Speedy justice: The Lord pleads your cause and executes judgment for you. You shall look upon His vindication.[29] God gives justice to you speedily.[30]

And after you have suffered a little while, the God of all grace, who has called you to His eternal glory in Christ, will Himself restore, confirm, strengthen, and establish you.

1 Peter 5:10 ESV

---

[17] Mark 13:11 NIV;
    cf. Matt 10:20
[18] Luke 21:15 NIV
[19] Rom 8:38 ESV
[20] Rom 8:35 NASB
[21] Rom 8:38 ESV
[22] Rom 8:39 ESV
[23] 2Thes 1:5 NIV

[24] 1Pet 5:10 ESV
[25] Gal 1:4 ESV
[26] Jer 23:4 ESV
[27] Ezek 34:28 NASB
[28] Heb 13:6 ESV
[29] Micah 7:9 ESV
    cf. Ezek 34:16
[30] Luke 18:7-8 ESV;

* *Literally,* brotherhood.

***Literally,* the Gentiles.

42. The Lord Bears You Up

My wife and I enjoy taking walks together, and the local shopping mall is handy on hot, cold, or rainy days. But between the finish on the mall floors, the soles of my wife's shoes, and the angle of her steps, her foot can suddenly grab and she can seriously stumble. We discovered that if she always holds my hand, however, she won't fall. Do you realize that God always holds your hand as you walk through life as His child? He supports you and keeps you from slipping or falling. At times he even carries you in His arms. When it comes to temptations, He sympathizes with your weaknesses, limits them, and provides you the way of escape. You are indeed in very good hands.

Lifted up: The Lord is your support,[1] and He lifts[2] and bears you up[3] and carries you[4] daily.[5] He upholds you[6] and your life,[7] and makes you to stand.[8] Your soul clings to the Lord God,[9] who takes you by the hand,[10] and upholds you with His righteous right hand.[11] You are in the Lord's hand,[12] and God's everlasting arms are underneath you.[13]

Kept from falling: The only God your Savior, through Jesus Christ your Lord,[14] keeps you from stumbling.[15] The angels of the Lord lift you up in their hands, so that you will not strike your foot against a stone.[16] The Lord makes your feet like the feet of a deer and sets you secure on the heights.[17] He will not let your foot slip.[18] The Lord's unfailing love supports you when your foot is slipping,[19] and He provides a broad path[20] for your feet, so that your ankles do not give way.[21] Though you may stumble, you will not fall, for the Lord upholds you with His hand.[22]

[1] 2Sam 22:19 NKJV
[2] Ps 147:6 NKJV; cf. Is 63:9
[3] Ps 68:19 ESV
[4] Is 63:9 ESV
[5] Ps 68:19 NASB; cf. Is 63:9
[6] Ps 37:17 NKJV; cf. Ps 41:12; 54:4; 94:18
[7] Ps 54:4 ESV
[8] Rom 14:4 NASB
[9] Ps 63:8 NASB
[10] Is 42:6 ESV
[11] Is 41:10 NKJV; cf. Ps 18:35; 63:8; 139:9-10
[12] Deut 33:3 NKJV
[13] Deut 33:27 NKJV
[14] Jude 1:25 NASB
[15] Jude 1:24 NASB; cf. Ps 116:8
[16] Ps 91:12 NIV
[17] 2Sam 22:34 ESV; cf. Hab 3:19
[18] Ps 121:3 NIV
[19] Ps 94:18 NIV
[20] 2Sam 22:37 NIV; cf. 2Sam 22:20
[21] 2Sam 22:37 NIV
[22] Ps 37:24 NIV

Enabled to resist temptation: Your Father in heaven does not lead you into temptation.[23] God never tempts you. He cannot be tempted by evil, nor does He tempt anyone.[24] God is faithful; He will not let you be tempted beyond what you can bear. But when you are tempted, He will also provide a way out so that you can endure it.[25] For you do not have a high priest who is unable to empathize with your weaknesses, but you have One who has been tempted in every way, just as you are—yet He did not sin.[26] Because Christ Himself has suffered when tempted, He is able to help you when you are being tempted.[27] The Lord has saved you from all your sinful backsliding, and has cleansed you.[28]

Blessed be the Lord,
who daily bears us up....
Psalm 68:19 ESV

---

[23] Matt 6:13;
  Luke 11:4 NKJV
[24] Jas 1:13 NIV

[25] 1Cor 10:13 NIV
[26] Heb 4:15 NIV
[27] Heb 2:18 ESV

[28] Ezek 37:23 NIV

43. God Sustains You

Some have envisioned God as the One who got the universe started, but who now just sits back and watches what happens as if it were a reality TV show. The fact is that in Christ, God actively preserves, sustains, and renews you moment-by-moment. He surrounds and protects you on all sides, and makes and keeps you effective in faith and life. He is actively with you each step along the way, until one day you share fully with Him in His victory.

Guarded: By God's power you are being guarded through faith for a salvation ready to be revealed in the last time.[1] The Lord is always before you,[2] for He is at your right hand so that you will not be shaken.[3] The angel of the Lord encamps around you,[4] and God commands His angels concerning you to guard you in all your ways.[5] The Lord will guard you from this generation forever.[6]

Encircled: The Lord Himself goes before you,[7] and the glory of the Lord is your rear guard.[8] He encircles you;[9] hems you in, behind and before; and lays His hand upon you.[10]

Preserved: The Lord preserves[11] and sustains you[12] forever.[13] His steadfast love and His faithfulness will ever preserve you![14] The Lord knows how[15] to preserve you from trouble.[16] Though you walk in the midst of trouble, it is the Lord who preserves your life.[17]

Kept vital: The Lord makes you like His majestic horse in battle.[18] You will soar on wings like an eagle; you will run and not grow weary, you will walk and not be faint.[19] God revives your spirit and heart.[20]

---

[1] 1Pet 1:5 ESV
[2] Acts 2:25 NIV
[3] Acts 2:25 NASB; cf. Ps 16:8
[4] Ps 34:7 NASB
[5] Ps 91:11 NIV
[6] Ps 12:7 ESV
[7] Deut 31:8 NIV
[8] Is 58:8 NASB
[9] Deut 32:10 NASB
[10] Ps 139:5 NIV
[11] Ps 31:23 ESV; cf. Ps 32:7; 37:28; 138:7; 145:20
[12] Ps 55:22 NASB
[13] Ps 37:28 NASB
[14] Ps 40:11 ESV
[15] 2Pet 2:9 ESV
[16] Ps 32:7 ESV; cf. 2Pet 2:9
[17] Ps 138:7 NIV
[18] Zech 10:3 NASB
[19] Is 40:31 NIV
[20] Is 57:15 NIV

Granted steadfast faith: Jesus prays for you, that your faith may not fail.[21] God's Word* is in your heart;[22] you walk in His name[23] and your steps do not slip.[24]

Made victorious: You have been born of God and you overcome the world. And this is the victory that has overcome the world—your faith.[25] God gives you the victory[26] through your Lord Jesus Christ.[27]

...by God's power [we] are being guarded through faith for a salvation ready to be revealed in the last time.

1 Peter 1:5 ESV

---

[21] Luke 22:32 NASB
[22] Ps 37:31 NASB
[23] Zech 10:12 ESV
[24] Ps 37:31 NASB

[25] 1John 5:4 ESV
[26] 1Cor 15:57 NASB; *cf.* Deut 20:4
[27] 1Cor 15:57 NASB

* *Literally*, The law of (your) God.

Today

You Are Being Transformed

Does your life as a Christian ever feel like you are stuck in a loop with little growth or change? God views your situation very differently. He is passionate about orchestrating your sanctification, and He is in the business of constantly transforming you from glory into glory. By the ongoing work of the Holy Spirit through God's Word, the amazing adventure that He has called you to continues to unfold. Welcome to the upward call of God in Christ Jesus![1]

44. Your Ongoing Sanctification

I've always enjoyed bumper stickers that read, "Please be patient—God isn't finished with me yet." God has a plan and process that He is masterfully carrying out in your life. Through His Spirit He gently exposes and deals with your pet sins. He disciplines you as a loving Father, helping you to grow and mature. He reminds you that He is God and you are not, humbling and reorienting you. He never runs ahead of you or lags behind. He is carrying out the perfect growing experience, and when it comes to you He never settles for second best. God be praised that you are still under construction!

Being renewed: God foreknew and predestined you to be conformed to the image of His Son.[2] Jesus is the founder and perfecter of your faith,[3] and your sanctification is God's will for you.[4] The Lord God gives you growth,[5] every moment[6] refining you as silver is refined,[7] and testing you as gold is tested.[8] Your inner self is being renewed day-by-day.[9] Together with all believers, you are being prepared[10] for the Lamb[11] as a bride beautifully dressed for her husband.[12] God sanctifies you[13] to manifest His holiness in you in the sight of all*.[14]

---

[1] Phil 3:14 ESV
[2] Rom 8:29 NKJV
[3] Heb 12:2 ESV
[4] 1Thes 4:3 NKJV
[5] 1Cor 3:6-7 ESV
[6] Job 7:18 NKJV
[7] Zech 13:9 NASB
[8] Zech 13:9 NASB; cf. Job 7:18
[9] 2Cor 4:16 ESV
[10] Rev 21:2 NIV
[11] Rev 21:9 NIV
[12] Rev 21:2 NIV
[13] Heb 2:11 NKJV; cf. Heb 10:14
[14] Ezek 20:41; 28:25 ESV

98

Disciplined as His beloved child: As a man disciplines the child[15] in whom he delights,[16] you are blessed that[17] the Lord loves you[18] and disciplines,[19] chastises,[20] and reproves you,[21] as He does every child whom He receives.[22] God disciplines you for your good, so that you may share His holiness.[23] His discipline yields the peaceful fruit of righteousness as you are being trained by it.[24]

Enabled to fear the Lord: The Lord has put the fear of Himself in your heart, so that you will not turn from Him.[25] He established His covenant with you[26] so that you will remember your sins and cover your mouth in silent shame, since He has forgiven you all that you have done.[27]

...our inner self is being renewed day by day.
2 Corinthians 4:16 ESV

---

[15] Deut 8:5; Prov 3:12 NASB;
[16] Prov 3:12 NASB
[17] Ps 94:12 NIV
[18] Heb 12:6 NASB; cf. Prov 3:12; Rev 3:19
[19] Deut 8:5; Heb 12:6; Rev 3:19

NASB; cf. Ps 94:12
[20] Heb 12:6 ESV
[21] Prov 3:12; Rev 3:19 NASB
[22] Heb 12:6 NASB
[23] Heb 12:10 NASB
[24] Heb 12:11 NASB
[25] Jer 32:40 NASB

[26] Ezek 16:62 NASB
[27] Ezek 16:63 NLT

* *Literally*, the nations/Gentiles.

45. Not a Debtor to Your Flesh

Let's talk about that matter of ongoing sin. You know you are fully forgiven in Christ, yet sin is still clearly present in your life. In John's first letter, he tells you that no one who is born of God continues to sin,[1] but also that if you claim to have no sin you call God a liar.[2] So which is it? Actually, *both* are true! As a Christian you no longer make a *practice* of deliberately sinning. *Continuing* in sin involves knowing but not caring that what you are doing offends God, and refusing to repent or change. In Christ, your slavery to sin has been broken, but the tendency for you to still sin out of weakness remains throughout your earthly life. Your Lord directs you to confess such sins to Him and to others, resulting in your forgiveness and cleansing.

No longer practicing sin: You are born of God, and you do not make a practice of sinning, for God's seed abides in you. You cannot[3] and do not[4] keep on sinning,[5] because you have been born of God.[6] Sin is no longer your master.[7] You do not have an obligation to the flesh, to live according to it,[8] but God gives you a spirit of self-control.[9]

Confessing sins of weakness: You do not deceive yourself by claiming to be without sin.[10] When you sin, Jesus Christ is your advocate with the Father.[11] He is a great,[12] merciful, and faithful[13] high priest[14] in the service of God,[15] who has ascended into heaven[16] to make atonement for your sins.[17] You acknowledge your sin to the Lord and do not cover up your iniquity. You say, "I will confess my transgressions to the Lord."[18]

Receiving God's forgiveness: The Lord is good and forgiving, a-bounding in steadfast love to you.[19] God is faithful and just to forgive

---

[1] 1John 3:9 NIV
[2] 1John 1:10 NIV
[3] 1John 3:9 ESV
[4] 1John 5:18 ESV
[5] 1John 3:9; 5:18 ESV
[6] 1John 3:9 NIV; *cf.* 1John 5:18
[7] Rom 6:14 NIV
[8] Rom 8:12 NIV
[9] 2Tim 1:7 ESV
[10] 1John 1:8 NIV
[11] 1John 2:1 NKJV
[12] Heb 4:14 NKJV
[13] Heb 2:17 NKJV
[14] Heb 2:17; 4:14 NKJV
[15] Heb 2:17 ESV
[16] Heb 4:14 NIV
[17] Heb 2:17 NIV
[18] Ps 32:5 NIV
[19] Ps 86:5 ESV

you your sins and to cleanse you from all unrighteousness.[20] Your Father in heaven forgives you your sins.[21]

For You, O Lord, are good and forgiving, abounding in steadfast love to all who call upon You.

Psalm 86:5 ESV

---

[20] 1John 1:9 NKJV

[21] Luke 11:4 NKJV; *cf.* 2Chron 7:14; Ps 32:5; Matt 6:12

46. Part of God's Household

You are growing as a member of God's family, learning to love those that God loves and to serve Jesus by serving them. God gives you special roles in each season of your life. Some of those roles may be familiar and similar to what you have done in the past, while other roles may be excitingly or uncomfortably new. But in any event, they are always valuable, fulfilling, and tailor-made by God just for you. Christ is a masterful builder of His holy Temple, and you are an integral and unique part of it.

One in Christ: You were baptized into one body and made to drink of one Spirit.[1] You are a fellow citizen with the saints.[2] The Lord, the God of Abraham, the God of Isaac, and the God of Jacob, is also your God.[3] You are part of the Lord's holy nation[4] and a member of His household.[5] You love whoever has been born of the Father.[6] You are a member of Christ's body,[7] and God arranges you in that body as He chooses.[8] Should you be required to leave house or family members for the sake of the kingdom of God, you will receive many times more in this time.[9]

Built into a temple: You are growing together with your fellow saints, built on the foundation of the apostles and prophets, Christ Jesus Himself being the Cornerstone.[10] Like a living stone you are being built up as part of a spiritual house.[11] In Christ the whole building, being fitted together, grows into a holy temple in the Lord. In Him you are also being built together for a dwelling place of God in the Spirit.[12]

---

[1] 1Cor 12:13 NASB
[2] Eph 2:19 NKJV
[3] Luke 20:37-38 NKJV
[4] Ex 19:6 NKJV
[5] Eph 2:19 NIV
[6] 1John 5:1 ESV
[7] 1Cor 12:27 NASB
[8] 1Cor 12:18 ESV
[9] Luke 18:29-30 ESV
[10] Eph 2:19-21 ESV
[11] 1Pet 2:5 ESV
[12] Eph 2:21-22 NKJV

Now, therefore, you are…
fellow citizens with the saints and
members of the household of God.
Ephesians 2:19 NKJV

47. New Realities

In Christ, all things are new for you! Among these is a wonderful freedom to pursue what pleases God, no longer out of fear or compulsion but simply because Christ has made it possible and you enjoy doing so. You experience true joy, a sustainable and transforming sense of peace and well-being far more wonderful than fleeting episodes of happiness. You are also being transformed from glory into glory, becoming more like Jesus, and you will ultimately shine forever in eternity with Him. Praise God for all the marvelous gifts with which He has blessed you!

True freedom: It was for freedom that Christ set you free.[1] You were called to be free,[2] and you are enabled to live as a free person.[3] You know God's truth, and God's truth has made you free.[4]

Fullness of joy: Your heart rejoices in the Lord,[5] and He is the One who lifts your head.[6] He increases your joy,[7] and in His presence you experience fullness of joy.[8] You have been filled by the God of hope with all joy in believing,[9] rejoicing in God[10] through your Lord Jesus Christ.[11] The Lord God keeps you occupied with joy in your heart,[12] more joy than people have when their grain and wine abound.[13]

Radiance: The Lord, who is your glory,[14] has glorified you.[15] From the Lord who is the Spirit, you behold the glory of the Lord and are being transformed into the same image from one degree of glory to another.[16] You look to the Lord and are radiant.[17] The name of our Lord Jesus is glorified in you, and you in Him, according to the grace of our God and the Lord Jesus Christ.[18]

---

[1] Gal 5:1 NASB
[2] Gal 5:13 NIV
[3] 1Pet 2:16 NIV
[4] John 8:32 NASB
[5] Ps 33:21 NASB
[6] Ps 3:3 NASB
[7] Is 9:3 NIV;
  cf. Eccl 2:26
[8] Ps 16:11 NKJV;
  cf. Acts 2:28
[9] Rom 15:13 NKJV
[10] Rom 5:11 NKJV;
  cf. Zech 10:7
[11] Rom 5:11 NKJV
[12] Eccl 5:20 ESV;
  cf. Ps 4:7
[13] Ps 4:7 ESV;
  cf. Zech 10:7
[14] Ps 3:3 NKJV;
  cf. Ps 62:7
[15] Is 55:5 NKJV
[16] 2Cor 3:18 ESV
[17] Ps 34:5 NIV
[18] 2Thes 1:12 NIV

...we constantly pray for you...
that the name of our Lord Jesus
may be glorified in you, and you in
Him, according to the grace of our
God and the Lord Jesus Christ.
2 Thessalonians 1:11-12 NIV

Today

You Experience New Life

So how does your Christian life appear to you? Do you seem to be merely making do or scraping by? If so, you could definitely benefit from new lenses. God has blessed you with every spiritual blessing in Christ, and He has put everything in place for you to live abundantly and to be fully satisfied. He supplies all you could need and withholds nothing from you. May you see with enhanced clarity the new life that God so lovingly and lavishly provides for you.

48. Blessed Abundantly

A few years ago, my wife began a Thanksgiving tradition with our extended family. We take turns around the table, sharing blessings for which each of us is thankful to God. It is always so encouraging to recall and celebrate the goodness of the Lord among us. Here you are invited to marvel anew at God's rich and abundant blessings to you. May you truly feast upon it!

Abundant life: The Spirit gives you[1] life[2] abundantly.[3] Just as Christ was raised from the dead by the glory of the Father, you now walk in newness of life.[4] The Lord your God blesses you[5] and pours out His blessing on you.[6] He satisfies[7] your desire[8] with His goodness[9] and it will be well with you.[10] God richly provides you with everything to enjoy.[11] You feast on the abundance of God's house; He gives you drink from His river of delights.[12]

Every spiritual blessing: The Lord has done great things for you.[13] God's divine power has granted to you all things that pertain to life and godliness, through the knowledge of Him who called you to His own glory and excellence.[14] He has blessed you with every spiritual blessing in the heavenly places in Christ.[15] The Lord has stored up

[1] 2Cor 3:6 NKJV
[2] 2Cor 3:6; John 10:10 NKJV
[3] John 10:10 NKJV
[4] Rom 6:4 ESV
[5] Ps 67:6; Num 6:24 NASB;
cf. Ps 34:8; Is 44:3; Luke 11:28
[6] Is 44:3 NASB
[7] Jer 31:14 NASB; *cf.* Is 58:11
[8] Is 58:11 NASB; *cf.* Ps 145:19
[9] Jer 31:14 NKJV
[10] Eccl 8:12 NKJV
[11] 1Tim 6:17 ESV
[12] Ps 36:8 NIV
[13] Ps 126:3 ESV
[14] 2Pet 1:3 ESV
[15] Eph 1:3 NASB

106

abundant goodness for you,[16] and He graciously[17] withholds no good thing from you.[18]

Your soul satisfied: The God of all grace Himself[19] restores[20] your soul.[21] He satisfies your longing soul, and fills your hungry soul with good things.[22] As you remember God, your soul is satisfied as with fat and rich food.[23]

[God's] divine power has granted to us all things that pertain to life and godliness, through the knowledge of Him who called us to His own glory and excellence.

2 Peter 1:3 ESV

---

[16] Ps 31:19 ESV
[17] Rom 8:32 NIV
[18] Ps 84:11 NIV;
  cf. Rom 8:32

[19] 1Pet 5:10 ESV
[20] Ps 23:3 ESV;
  cf. 1Pet 5:10
[21] Ps 23:3 ESV

[22] Ps 107:9 ESV
[23] Ps 63:5-6 ESV

49. Physical Needs Supplied

> God knows you need food, clothes, shelter, and health to function in this world. After all, He made you the way you are, and Jesus personally experienced all these same needs as He lived among us. Jesus assures you that, as you seek what is important to God, God commits Himself to meeting your physical needs as well. He often satisfies these needs through your productive work, regular exercise, and healthy lifestyle, as all along you look to Him as your Provider and Great Physician.

All needs met: Because the Lord is your Shepherd, you lack nothing.[1] God meets all your needs according to the riches of His glory in Christ Jesus.[2]

Parables of provision: Consider the ravens of the air: they do not sow or reap, they have no storeroom or barn, and yet your heavenly Father feeds them. And how much more valuable you are than birds![3] Consider how the wild flowers grow. They do not labor or spin. Yet Jesus tells you that not even Solomon in all his splendor was dressed like one of these. If that is how God clothes the grass of the field, which is here today and tomorrow is thrown into the fire, will He not much more clothe you![4] Your heavenly Father knows that you need these, and as you are seeking first His kingdom and His righteousness, all these things will be given to you as well.[5]

Hunger and thirst satisfied: That you should eat and drink and take pleasure in all your toil—this is God's gift to you.[6] The Lord makes you lie down in green pastures and leads you beside quiet waters.[7] He prepares a table before you in the presence of your enemies; your cup overflows.[8] The Lord is as one who lifts the yoke from your jaws; and He bends down to you[9] and feeds you Himself.[10] Your Father in heaven[11] provides food for you[12] each day[13] and will fill your mouth.[14]

[1] Ps 23:1 NIV
[2] Phil 4:19 NIV
[3] Luke 12:24; Matt 6:26 NIV
[4] Luke 12:27-28; Matt 6:28-30 NIV
[5] Luke 12:30-31; Matt 6:32-33 NIV
[6] Eccl 3:13 ESV
[7] Ps 23:2 NIV
[8] Ps 23:5 NIV
[9] Hos 11:4 NASB
[10] Ezek 34:23 NASB; cf. Hos 11:4
[11] Matt 6:9 NIV; cf. Luke 11:2
[12] Ps 111:5 NIV; cf. Matt 6:11; Luke 11:3
[13] Luke 11:3 NASB; cf. Matt 6:11
[14] Ps 81:10 NASB

The Lord feeds you with the finest of the wheat, and with honey from the rock the Lord satisfies you.[15] You are to go and eat your food with gladness, and drink your cup* with a joyful heart, for God has already approved what you do.[16]

Life and Health addressed: The Lord is your life and the length of your days.[17] He is your healer.[18] It is the Lord that sustains you on your sickbed and restores you to health.[19] He satisfies you with good so that your youth is renewed like the eagle's.[20] The Lord leads you to rest[21] and gives to you, His beloved, sleep.[22]

Home blessed: It is the Lord who blesses your home[23] with peace.[24]

And my God will meet all your needs according to the riches of His glory in Christ Jesus.
Philippians 4:19 NIV

[15] Ps 81:16 NASB
[16] Eccl 9:7 NIV
[17] Deut 30:20 NKJV;
   cf. Ps 91:16
[18] Ex 15:26 ESV;
   cf. Ps 103:3
[19] Ps 41:3 NASB
[20] Ps 103:5 ESV
[21] Ezek 34:15 NASB
[22] Ps 127:2 ESV
[23] Prov 3:33 NKJV
[24] Luke 10:5 NKJV

* *Literally,* wine.

50. Filled with the Fullness of God

I recall once attempting to double the recipe for a batch of brownies. I am still not fully certain what happened, but I know the result was definitely *not* brownies. When God fills you with His fullness, He never gives you less than the full portion. The Bread of Life and the living water that He provides is always more than enough. He gives all of Himself to you, so that the finished product is exactly what He promises. In the hands of the Master Baker, you are coming out just right!

Sharing in Christ: You have come to share in Christ.[1] You are being filled with all the fullness of God[2] and you know every good thing that is in you for Christ's sake.[3]

Living water: Your fountain of life is with God.[4] You drink the water that Christ gives you, so you will never be thirsty again.[5] Out of your heart flow rivers of living water,[6] and you are like a well-watered garden, like a spring whose waters never fail.[7]

Bread of Life: You have come to Jesus, the Bread of Life, and you will not hunger and will never thirst.[8] You abide in Christ,[9] the living Bread that came down from heaven,[10] and He abides in you.[11] And so you eat[12] and drink Christ,[13] feeding on the true food of His flesh and drinking the true drink of His blood.[14]

[1] Heb 3:14 NIV
[2] Eph 3:19 NKJV
[3] Phm 1:6 NASB
[4] Ps 36:9 NASB
[5] John 4:14 ESV
[6] John 7:38 NKJV
[7] Is 58:11 NIV
[8] John 6:35 NASB
[9] John 6:56 NASB
[10] John 6:51 NIV; cf. John 6:58
[11] John 6:56 NASB
[12] John 6:51 NASB; cf. John 6:53-56, 58
[13] John 6:53-56 NASB
[14] John 6:55-57 NASB

For this reason I bow my knees to the Father...that you may be filled with all the fullness of God.
Ephesians 3:14-19 NKJV

51. Given Every Good Gift

What is your "love language?" God is fluent in them all! When it comes to gift giving, no one can compare. He's absolutely in a league of His own. He gives abundantly, consistently, and irrevocably. He keeps His promises without fail. He gives you rest from the impossible demands of the Law. He provides times of refreshing for you. He honors and exalts you. What surprise token of His love is on its way to you this very day? I'll bet you can't wait to find out!

Gifts from above: Every good thing given and every perfect gift is from above, coming down to you from the Father of lights, with whom there is no variation or shifting shadow.[1] Grace was given to you according to the measure of Christ's gift,[2] and from Christ's fullness you have received, grace upon grace.[3] God makes all grace abound to you.[4]

Sabbath rest: There is a Sabbath rest for you,[5] and you have entered God's rest,[6] just as He promised.[7] The Lord God gives you relief when you are in distress[8] and rest from days of trouble.[9]

Honored and exalted: The Lord bestows His riches on you.[10] For your sake our Lord Jesus Christ became poor, so that through Christ's poverty you might become rich.[11] The Lord honors[12] and exalts you.[13] See, your Savior comes! See, His reward is with Him, and His recompense accompanies Him.[14]

[1] Jas 1:17 NASB
[2] Eph 4:7 ESV
[3] John 1:16 ESV
[4] 2Cor 9:8 NASB
[5] Heb 4:9 NASB
[6] Heb 4:3 NASB; cf. Heb 4:1,9
[7] Heb 4:1 NASB
[8] Ps 4:1 ESV
[9] Ps 94:13 ESV
[10] Rom 10:12 ESV
[11] 2Cor 8:9 NIV
[12] Ps 91:15 NIV
[13] Ps 37:34 NIV; cf. Luke 18:14
[14] Is 62:11 NIV

Every good and perfect gift is from above, coming down from the Father of the heavenly lights, who does not change like shifting shadows.

James 1:17 NIV

You Are Blessed to Serve

With the prospect of perfect joy in heaven, why in the world are you still here in the world? It's because He has important work for you to do here!

52. Given Purpose

> You have been commissioned to carry on God's gracious work on earth—to lead others to Him and to help and support your brothers and sisters in Christ. He has enough confidence in you (actually Himself), that He entrusts you with carrying out His plan of extending the reach of His love and kindness here. When He welcomes you one day to His home forever, oh, the stories we will have to share and enjoy about how God blessed others through you!

Called with purpose: God causes all things to work together for good for you, who are called according to His purpose.[1] You share in a heavenly calling with all believers,[2] and the Lord God Most High fulfills His purpose for you.[3] The Lord knows the plans He has for you, plans for welfare and not for evil, to give you a future and a hope.[4] Your inheritance will endure forever.[5] For you God's call is irrevocable.[6]

In Christ's service: You serve the Lord Christ.[7] You are released from the law, having died to that which held you captive, so that you serve in the new way of the Spirit and not in the old way of the written code.[8] As you lose your life for Christ's sake and the gospel's, you save it.[9] The sharing of your faith is effective for the sake of Christ.[10]

Stewardship: God made you in His own image, after His likeness,[11] and He directs you to rule over the fish in the sea and the birds in the sky and over every living creature that moves on the ground.[12] You use the gift you have received to serve others, as a faithful steward of

---

[1] Rom 8:28 NASB
[2] Heb 3:1 ESV
[3] Ps 57:2; 138:8 ESV
[4] Jer 29:11 ESV
[5] Ps 37:18 NIV
[6] Rom 11:29 NIV
[7] Col 3:24 NKJV
[8] Rom 7:6 ESV
[9] Mark 8:35 ESV
[10] Phm 1:6 ESV
[11] Gen 1:26-27 ESV
[12] Gen 1:28,26 NIV

His grace in its various forms.[13] God, like a man going on a journey, entrusts His wealth to you[14] according to your own ability,[15] and you trade[16] and make more for Him.[17] He says to you, "Well done, good and faithful servant! You have been faithful with a few things; I will put you in charge of many things."[18] For to you who have, more will be given,[19] and you will have an abundance.[20]

The Lord will fulfill His purpose for me; Your steadfast love, O Lord, endures forever....

Psalm 138:8 ESV

---

[13] 1Pet 4:10 NIV
[14] Matt 25:14 NIV; *cf.* Luke 19:13
[15] Matt 25:15 NKJV
[16] Matt 25:16 NKJV; *cf.* Matt 25:17; Luke 19:13

[17] Matt 25:16 NKJV; *cf.* Luke 19:16,18
[18] Matt 25:21,23 NIV; *cf.* Luke 19:17,19

[19] Luke 19:26 NIV; *cf.* Matt 25:29; Mark 4:24-25
[20] Matt 25:29 NIV

53. Productive Life

> One morning I walked around the corner and discovered that my neighbor's massive tree had been uprooted by strong winds during the night and was now lying on the ground. The roots that once anchored the tree and provided it with water and nourishment were now exposed. I knew that all its green leaves would soon turn brown and fall off. What a chilling image of life apart from Christ! But in Christ you are like a tree securely planted by a constant water source. You are enabled to produce an abundance of fruit—serving and blessing others. And Jesus as your Master Gardener is always helping you bear even more fruit.

Bearing fruit: The Lord saves you, and you will be a blessing.[1] Jesus chose you and appointed you that you would go and bear fruit, and that your fruit would remain.[2] You abide in Jesus and He abides in you,[3] and you have died to the law through the body of Christ, in order that you may bear fruit for God.[4] And so you are bearing much fruit[5] with patience;[6] and together with your fellow believers*, you are filling the whole world with fruit.[7]

Like a fruitful tree: You are like a tree planted by streams of water[8] that sends out its roots by the stream,[9] blossoms, and sprouts.[10] You do not fear when heat comes and you have no worries in a year of drought. Your leaves are always green[11] and do not wither.[12] You do not cease from[13] yielding fruit[14] in season.[15] You flourish like the grain and you blossom like the vine—your fame is like the wine of Lebanon.[16] Jesus is pruning you so that you will be even more fruitful.[17] You are growing and are yielding fruit a hundredfold.[18] You still bear fruit in old age; you are ever full of sap and green, to declare that the Lord is upright.[19]

---

[1] Zech 8:13 ESV
[2] John 15:16 NASB
[3] John 15:5 NASB
[4] Rom 7:4 ESV
[5] John 15:5 NKJV;
 cf. Luke 8:15
[6] Luke 8:15 NKJV
[7] Is 27:6 NASB

[8] Ps 1:3 NIV;
 cf. Jer 17:8
[9] Jer 17:8 NIV;
 cf. Is 27:6
[10] Is 27:6 NASB
[11] Jer 17:8 NIV
[12] Ps 1:3 NIV
[13] Jer 17:8 NKJV

[14] Jer 17:8 NKJV;
 cf. Ps 1:3
[15] Ps 1:3 NIV
[16] Hos 14:7 NIV
[17] John 15:2 NIV
[18] Luke 8:8;
 Matt 13:23 ESV
[19] Ps 92:14-15 ESV

Fruit of the Spirit: The fruit of the Spirit in you is love, joy, peace, patience, kindness, goodness, faithfulness, gentleness, and self-control.[20] You love because God first loved you.[21] God gave you a spirit of love and self-control.[22] He makes your love increase and overflow for your fellow believers** and for everyone else.[23] You are rooted and grounded in love,[24] and in you truly the love of God is perfected.[25] He comforts you in all your troubles, so that you can comfort those in any trouble with the comfort you yourself receive from Him.[26] God reconciled you to Himself through Christ and gave you the ministry of reconciliation.[27]

"You did not choose Me but I chose you, and appointed you that you would go and bear fruit, and that your fruit would remain...."

John 15:16 NASB

[20] Gal 5:22-23 NASB
[21] 1John 4:19 NASB
[22] 2Tim 1:7 ESV
[23] 1Thes 3:12 NIV
[24] Eph 3:17 NKJV
[25] 1John 2:5 ESV
[26] 2Cor 1:3-4 NIV
[27] 2Cor 5:18 NIV

* *Literally,* Jacob...they.

** *Literally,* each other.

54. God Working Through You

As my wife and I walked up to the hospital where my daughter was to be born, I was shocked by its massive, 10-foot-tall, wooden front doors. I wondered aloud, "How could a sick person ever get into this place?" But when I reached to open the door, it swung open easily with the help of a power-assist motor. I realized this is similar to what happens when you act in faith on God's commands. The works that God wants you to accomplish may seem daunting, but the power of the Holy Spirit within you enables you to carry out whatever He asks of you. He chooses good works for you to do, He prepares them in advance, He creates in you the desire to do them, and He Himself does them through you. So don't be afraid to reach out and open that door!

Doing the works of Christ: You have become a slave to righteousness[1] and of God.[2] You are doing the works that Jesus Christ did, and you will do even greater things than these, because He has gone to the Father.[3] The Lord makes you a blessing.[4] Jesus declares that you are the salt of the earth[5] and the light of the world.[6] At one time you were darkness, but now you are light in the Lord.[7]

God makes it happen: God thoroughly equips you[8] so that you will abound[9] in every good work[10] and be made complete through the Scripture.[11] The Lord has indeed done for you all your works.[12] You are God's workmanship, created in Christ Jesus for good works, which God prepared beforehand that you should walk in them.[13] The God of peace[14] is working in you,[15] both to will and to do[16] what is well pleasing in His sight,[17] through Jesus Christ.[18] It is our Lord Jesus Christ Himself, and your God and Father, that establish you in every good word and work,[19] and Jesus purifies you to be zealous for good

---

[1] Rom 6:18 NIV
[2] Rom 6:22 NIV
[3] John 14:12 NIV
[4] Ezek 34:26 NASB
[5] Matt 5:13 NASB
[6] Matt 5:14 NASB
[7] Eph 5:8 ESV
[8] 2Tim 3:17 NKJV
[9] 2Cor 9:8 NIV
[10] 2Cor 9:8 NIV; cf. 2Tim 3:17
[11] 2Tim 3:16-17 ESV
[12] Is 26:12 ESV
[13] Eph 2:10 NKJV
[14] Heb 13:20 NKJV
[15] Heb 13:21 NKJV; cf. Phil 2:13
[16] Phil 2:13 NKJV
[17] Heb 13:21 NKJV; cf. Phil 2:13
[18] Heb 13:21 NKJV
[19] 2Thes 2:16-17 NKJV

works.[20] God fulfills in you every resolve for good and every work of faith by His power.[21] In the Lord your labor is not in vain,[22] and whatever you do prospers.[23]

... for it is God who works in you,
both to will and to work
for His good pleasure.
Phil 2:13 ESV

---

[20] Tit 2:14 NKJV

[21] 2Thes 1:11 ESV

[22] 1Cor 15:58 ESV

[23] Ps 1:3 NIV

55. His Power at Work in You

During a power failure in your home, your microwave becomes just another cabinet and your TV a rather poor mirror. They only fulfill their intended purposes when plugged into a live power source. I've heard Christians talk about their need to "re-charge their spiritual batteries." By attending the vital gift of Sunday morning worship and perhaps a nourishing midweek service or Bible study, they hope to store up enough power to function through the rest of the week. But one day as I was meditating on John 15:5, where Jesus declares that apart from Him we can do *nothing*, I realized that you and I don't have batteries! Power only flows through you as you are connected to *Him*—your power Source. In Christ you have been provided unlimited access to God's limitless power at all times—the very same power that raised Jesus from the dead! And by God's grace you remain securely plugged in.

Clothed with power: Christ is the power of God to you,[1] and God gives you a spirit of power.[2] You know the power of Jesus' resurrection[3] and God's incomparably great power for you. That power is the same as the mighty strength God exerted when He raised Christ from the dead and seated Him at His right hand in the heavenly realms.[4] You have been clothed with power from on high,[5] and God is able to do immeasurably more than all that you ask or imagine, according to His power that is at work within you.[6] Your awesome God gives power to you[7] and equips you[8] with increased[9] strength.[10] The Lord's grace is sufficient for you, for His power is made perfect in your weakness.[11]

Holy Spirit within: You have received the promised gift of the Holy Spirit from the Lord your God,[12] who poured out His Spirit on you[13] and put His Holy Spirit in your midst.[14] God's love has been poured into your heart through the Holy Spirit who has been given to you.[15]

---

[1] 1Cor 1:24 NASB
[2] 2Tim 1:7 NASB
[3] Phil 3:10 NASB
[4] Eph 1:19-20 NIV
[5] Luke 24:49 NIV
[6] Eph 3:20 NIV
[7] Ps 68:35 NIV

[8] Ps 18:32 ESV;
cf. Ps 68:35;
Is 40:29
[9] Is 40:29 NKJV
[10] Ps 18:32; Is 40:29 NKJV;
cf. Ps 68:35
[11] 2Cor 12:9 NIV

[12] Acts 2:38-39 NASB;
cf. 1Thes 4:8
[13] Is 44:3 NASB;
cf. Luke 24:49
[14] Is 63:11 NASB
[15] Rom 5:5 ESV

You have been strengthened with power through the Father's Spirit in your inner being.[16]

Uniquely gifted: According to the grace given to you,[17] you have received your own special gift from God.[18] His gifts to you are irrevocable.[19] The manifestation of the Spirit is given to you for the common good,[20] and you have the firstfruits of the Spirit.[21]

Enabled to do all things: Christ is powerful in dealing with you.[22] All things are possible for you,[23] and you can do all things through Christ who strengthens you.[24] God makes you have all sufficiency in all things at all times.[25]

[God] is able to do immeasurably more than all we ask or imagine, according to His power that is at work in us.

Ephesians 3:20 NIV

---

[16] Eph 3:16 NIV
[17] Rom 12:6 NASB
[18] 1Cor 7:7;
  1Pet 4:10 NASB;
  cf. Rom 12:6
[19] Rom 11:29 NASB
[20] 1Cor 12:7 NASB
[21] Rom 8:23 NASB
[22] 2Cor 13:3 NIV
[23] Mark 9:23 ESV
[24] Phil 4:13 NASB
[25] 2Cor 9:8 ESV

56. Worshiping in Spirit and Truth

You were created, redeemed, and empowered so that God is glorified in you and your life. Worship and praise are your expressions of love and appreciation to your wonderful God, who loves you and gave His Son for you. You join freely and gladly in worship with your brothers and sisters in Christ. He fills you with songs of praise and thanksgiving, and you sing for joy (or at least make a "joyful noise"). You share Christ's wondrous meal, to which He personally invites you. All of these are but a wonderful foretaste of the ultimate worship, the glorious music, and the heavenly banquet yet to come!

Purposed for worship: In Christ, the God and Father of your Lord Jesus Christ blessed you with every spiritual blessing,[1] chose you to be holy and blameless before Him,[2] and adopted you as His child;[3] Jesus Christ, the Beloved,[4] redeemed you through His blood, forgives your trespasses,[5] and makes known to you the mystery of His will;[6] and the Holy Spirit, with whom you were sealed, is the guarantee of[7] the inheritance[8] you have obtained in Christ[9] until you acquire possession of it[10]—all this to the praise of God's glory[11] and His glorious grace.[12] You are being built up to offer spiritual sacrifices acceptable to God through Jesus Christ.[13] As God's power works within you, glory is given to God.[14] You offer to Him[15] acceptable[16] worship[17] in spirit and truth,[18] with reverence and awe.[19] God is holy, enthroned upon your praises.[20]

Given songs of praise: The Lord is your song[21] and your praise.[22] God gives you songs in the night.[23] He puts a new song in your mouth, a song of praise to your God.[24] In the shadow of God's wings[25] you sing for joy.[26]

[1] Eph 1:3 ESV
[2] Eph 1:4 NASB
[3] Eph 1:5 NASB
[4] Eph 1:6 NASB
[5] Eph 1:7 NASB
[6] Eph 1:9 NASB
[7] Eph 1:13-14 ESV
[8] Eph 1:11,14 NKJV
[9] Eph 1:11 NKJV
[10] Eph 1:14 ESV
[11] Eph 1:12,14 NASB
[12] Eph 1:6 NIV
[13] 1Pet 2:5 ESV
[14] Eph 3:20-21 NASB
[15] Heb 12:28 NASB; cf. John 4:24
[16] Heb 12:28 NASB
[17] Heb 12:28 ESV; cf. John 4:24
[18] John 4:24 NASB
[19] Heb 12:28 NASB
[20] Ps 22:3 NASB
[21] Ex 15:2 NASB; cf. Ps 118:14
[22] Deut 10:21 NASB
[23] Job 35:10 NASB
[24] Ps 40:3 NASB
[25] Ps 63:7 NASB; cf. Ps 36:7
[26] Ps 63:7 NASB

Invited to the Lord's Supper: Jesus gives you bread, saying to you that this is His body,[27] which is given for you.[28] In the same way[29] He gives you to drink from the cup,[30] saying to you that this cup[31] is the new covenant in His blood,[32] which is poured out for you[33] for the forgiveness of sins.[34] These help you to keep your mind stayed on Him[35] and to proclaim the Lord's death until He comes.[36]

[The Lord] put a new song in my mouth, a song of praise to our God....

Psalm 40:3 NASB

---

[27] Matt 26:26 NKJV; cf. Mark 14:22; Luke 22:19; 1Cor 11:23-24
[28] Luke 22:19 NKJV; cf. 1Cor 11:24
[29] 1Cor 11:25 NASB
[30] Matt 26:27 NASB; cf. Mark 14:23
[31] Luke 22:20 NASB; cf. 1Cor 11:25
[32] Luke 22:20; 1Cor 11:25 NASB; cf. Matt 26:28; Mark 14:24
[33] Matt 26:28 NIV; cf. Mark 14:24
[34] Matt 26:28 NIV
[35] Is 26:3 NKJV; cf. Luke 22:19; 1Cor 11:24-25; Rom 8:6
[36] 1Cor 11:26 NASB

That You May Know

FOREVER
You know the riches of God's glorious inheritance in you.[1]

During tough or disappointing situations, I like to share two things that I know for sure: 1) I am going to heaven, and 2) this isn't it. Outside of funerals, most people don't talk much about death and heaven. The 1st-century world Jesus entered wasn't much different. But Jesus extensively interjected into His conversations with people the topics of death, His return, and the life to come. You will find Him addressing such topics in over one-third of the "red letter" (Jesus speaking) verses in the Gospel of Matthew, and in nearly one-half of all His recorded parables.

As real and tangible as this physical universe appears, Jesus reminds you that it is all only temporary. Instead of loving the world and the things in it, His earnest desire is for you to set your heart instead on the things above. Because of infection with sin, all creation groans as it eagerly awaits our transformation at Christ's return and the revealing of the new heavens and new earth.

In your journey through God's remarkable promises and assurances, you have seen God's faithfulness both *yesterday* and *today*. By the working of God's Spirit, you are enabled to have the same confidence in the promises and assurances yet to be fulfilled. In the following pages you will review all God has revealed to you about the perfect, sin-free kingdom that awaits. Each day brings you closer to experiencing all He has promised you. It could be today!

---

[1] Eph 1:18 ESV

Hope That Doesn't Disappoint

You probably know what it is like to be let down by someone you trusted. You feel so hurt and violated. God offers you a very different kind of hope. He has demonstrated His perfect faithfulness, so that you are learning to trust Him unconditionally. You can be equally confident about everything He promises you that is yet to be fulfilled. Though all others fail you, God cannot and will not fail you!

57. The Hope That Is in You

We often use the word *hope* casually today, like wishing (*I hope the rain holds off*) or politely asking (*I hope you don't mind*). But in the Bible, *hope* refers to confident, bet-your-life expectation for a future event or situation. As a believer your life is based on and defined by hope—hope for forgiveness, hope for redemption, hope for access to heaven. God's Word proclaims these precious promises and the Holy Spirit enables you to rely upon them. The Lord has repeatedly proven to you His faithfulness, and He has given you His Holy Spirit as a pledge of assurance that all of His wonderful promises to you will be perfectly fulfilled.

Hope abounds: Through Christ your hope is[1] from[2] and in[3] the Lord.[4] God your Father has given you good hope through grace.[5] You hope in Jesus' name.[6] The Lord is your portion and therefore you hope in Him.[7] The Lord God is an everlasting rock for you.[8] The Lord has es-tablished you forever.[9] You have been made an heir according to the hope of eternal life.[10] Christ in you is your hope of glory.[11] Through Jesus Christ you rejoice in hope of the glory of God,[12] and such hope does not disappoint.[13]

[1] 1Pet 1:21 NASB
[2] Ps 62:5 NASB
[3] Ps 39:7 NASB; cf. 1Pet 1:21
[4] Ps 39:7 NASB; cf. Ps 62:5; 1Pet 1:21
[5] 2Thes 2:16 ESV
[6] Matt 12:21 NASB
[7] Lam 3:24 NKJV
[8] Is 26:4 ESV
[9] 2Chron 9:8 NASB
[10] Tit 3:7 NASB
[11] Col 1:27 NKJV
[12] Rom 5:2 NKJV
[13] Rom 5:5 NKJV

Enrolled in heaven: Your name is written in heaven[14]—written before the foundation of the world in the book of life of the Lamb who was slain.[15] Jesus Christ will never blot out your name from His book.[16] At the time of the end you, whose name shall be found written in the book, shall be delivered.[17] You have been registered in heaven,[18] where you have citizenship.[19]

Guaranteed inheritance: God chose your inheritance for you.[20] You were sealed for the day of redemption by the Holy Spirit of God,[21] whom God gave you[22] as a guarantee of your inheritance until you acquire possession of it.[23] You are to inherit salvation.[24]

... Christ in you [is]
the hope of glory.
Colossians 1:27 NKJV

---

[14] Luke 10:20 NKJV
[15] Rev 13:8 ESV;
  cf. Rev 20:15
[16] Rev 3:5 NIV
[17] Dan 12:1 ESV
[18] Heb 12:23 NKJV

[19] Phil 3:20 NKJV
[20] Ps 47:4 NIV
[21] Eph 4:30 NASB;
  cf. 2Cor 1:22; 5:5;
  Eph 1:13

[22] 2Cor 5:5 NASB;
  cf. 2Cor 1:22
[23] Eph 1:14 ESV;
  cf. 2Cor 1:22; 5:5
[24] Heb 1:14 ESV

58. Endless Confidence

> Will you make it to heaven? What if you don't remain faithful to the end? What if you fall short, losing interest or focus? If the outcome depended entirely on *you*, your prospects would indeed be hopeless. But since your hope is in *Christ,* you are completely secure because *He* is perfectly dependable. It's not that someday you will enter eternal life—you're already there! Because *He* is mighty and faithful, *you* can have unwavering confidence.

Sustained to the end: God, who began a good work in you,[1] will bring it to completion[2] at the coming of our Lord Jesus Christ.[3] God who calls you is faithful; He will surely do it.[4] You have been set free from sin and have become God's servant*, the fruit of which leads to[5] your complete sanctification[6] and its end, eternal life from the Spirit.[7] The Lord will establish your heart[8] and sustain you guiltless to the end.[9] He will keep you from stumbling, and present[10] your whole spirit,[11] heart,[12] soul, and body[13] blameless[14] in holiness[15] before the presence of His glory with great joy.[16] The tested genuineness of your faith—more precious than gold that perishes though it is tested by fire—will be found to result in praise and glory and honor at the revelation of Jesus Christ.[17] You have confidence in the day of judgment, because as Christ is, so also are you in this world.[18]

Eternal life now: Eternal life—you were called to this,[19] you believe in Jesus Christ for it,[20] and you know that you already have it.[21] You have passed from death to life.[22] The Father gave you to Jesus,[23] and

---

[1] Phil 1:6 NASB
[2] Phil 1:6 ESV; *cf.* 1Thes 5:23
[3] 1Thes 5:23 ESV
[4] 1Thes 5:24 ESV; *cf.* 1Cor 1:9
[5] Rom 6:22 ESV
[6] 1Thes 5:23 NKJV; *cf.* Rom 6:22
[7] Gal 6:8 NASB; *cf.* Rom 6:22
[8] 1Thes 3:13 NASB; *cf.* 1Cor 1:8
[9] 1Cor 1:8 ESV; *cf.* 1Thes 3:13
[10] Jude 1:24 NKJV
[11] 1Thes 5:23 NKJV
[12] 1Thes 3:13 NKJV
[13] 1Thes 5:23 NKJV
[14] 1Thes 3:13 NKJV; *cf.* 1Thes 5:23; Jude 1:24
[15] 1Thes 3:13 NKJV
[16] Jude 1:24 ESV; *cf.* 1Thes 3:13; 1Pet 1:8
[17] 1Pet 1:7 ESV
[18] 1John 4:17 NASB
[19] 1Tim 6:12 NASB
[20] 1Tim 1:16 NASB
[21] 1John 5:13 NIV; *cf.* John 3:36; 5:24; 6:54
[22] John 5:24 ESV
[23] John 17:2 NIV

Jesus gives you eternal life.[24] The living water that Christ gives to you has become in you a spring of water welling up to eternal life.[25] You eat[26] the true food[27] of Jesus's flesh,[28] the living bread that came down from heaven,[29] and you drink[30] the true drink[31] of His blood.[32] You therefore have eternal life, and Jesus Himself will raise you up on the last day.[33] No one will snatch you out of His hand. Jesus' Father, who has given you to Him, is greater than all; and no one is able to snatch you out of His Father's hand.[34]

...our Lord Jesus Christ...will sustain you to the end, guiltless in the day of our Lord Jesus Christ.
1 Corinthians 1:7-8 ESV

---

[24] John 10:28 NIV; cf. John 17:2

[25] John 4:10,14 NIV

[26] John 6:54,56 NIV; cf. John 6:57-58

[27] John 6:55 NASB

[28] John 6:54-56 NKJV; cf. John 6:57

[29] John 6:51 NKJV

[30] John 6:54,56 NKJV

[31] John 6:55 NASB

[32] John 6:54-56 NASB

[33] John 6:54 NASB

[34] John 10:28-29 NKJV

* *Literally*, slave.

59. Awaiting with Eager Anticipation

Most of us typically live and function in the present. But sometimes you may be looking forward to a special vacation—
perhaps in the mountains, along a beach, or to another country.
As you wait and anticipate, you still perform your everyday
tasks, activities, and job. But the upcoming vacation-of-a-life-
time impacts your mood, thoughts, and perspective. You may
walk with an extra spring in your step. You enjoy looking forward to this vacation in conversations with your fellow
travelers. How much more can you anticipate life eternal—
walking with God in the new perfect heavens and earth and experiencing absolute joy!

For Christ's return: You eagerly[1] await[2] a Savior[3] from heaven,[4] the
Lord Jesus Christ[5]—God's Son, whom He raised from the dead.[6] He
will give you some of the hidden manna*[7]—Christ Himself.[8] Your
Lord is coming,[9] and He will appear a second time to save you.[10] You
are not in darkness for the Day of the Lord to surprise you like a thief
in the night.[11]

For salvation: It will be said on the day that the Lord God swallows
up death forever and wipes every tear from your face, "Behold, this is
your God; you have waited for Him, that He might save you. This is
the Lord; you have waited for Him; you are glad and rejoice in His
salvation."[12]

For heaven: By faith through the Spirit, you eagerly[13] wait for[14] the
Lord's promise of new heavens and a new earth[15] in which righteousness dwells.[16] Your light momentary affliction is preparing for you an
eternal weight of glory beyond all comparison, as you look not to the
things that are seen but to the things that are unseen. For the things

---

[1] Heb 9:28 NASB
[2] Heb 9:28 NASB;
  cf. Phil 3:20;
  1Thes 1:10
[3] Phil 3:20 NASB
[4] 1Thes 1:10 NASB;
  cf. Phil 3:20
[5] Phil 3:20 NASB;
  cf. 1Thes 1:10;
  Heb 9:28
[6] 1Thes 1:10 NASB
[7] Rev 2:17 NASB
[8] John 6:51 NASB;
  cf. John 6:48-50
[9] Matt 24:42 NASB
[10] Heb 9:28 ESV
[11] 1Thes 5:2,4 ESV
[12] Is 25:8-9 ESV
[13] Gal 5:5 ESV
[14] Gal 5:5 ESV;
  cf. 2Pet 3:13
[15] 2Pet 3:13 NKJV
[16] 2Pet 3:13 NKJV;
  cf. Gal 5:5

that are seen are transient, but the things that are unseen are eternal.[17] And after you have suffered a little while, the God of all grace, who has called you to His eternal glory in Christ, will Himself restore, confirm, strengthen, and establish you.[18]

*But our citizenship is in heaven,
and from it we await a Savior,
the Lord Jesus Christ.*

Philippians 3:20 ESV

---

[17] 2Cor 4:17-18 ESV
[18] 1Pet 5:10 ESV

* See *manna, hidden* in glossary.

60. Waiting to Be Changed

A few Thanksgivings ago, I was playing touch football with my sons-in-law and their brothers and friends. After finding myself on the ground repeatedly, I came to the brilliant conclusion that I should probably retire from playing football. Perhaps you are now young and vital, but you know such things are liable to change over time. Today I can enjoy a 15-mile walk, but in the not-too-distant future it may be a major accomplishment for me to get to the mailbox and back. In this fallen world, perhaps you entered life with a disability or have since been diagnosed with a chronic condition. Regardless, everyone who is Christ has this fact in common—we shall all be changed. You will be getting a new, glorified body like the body of the resurrected Christ! How amazing is that?

Transformed body: You wait eagerly for the redemption of your body.[1] For you know that if the earthly tent you live in is destroyed, you have a building from God, an eternal house in heaven, not built by human hands. Meanwhile you groan, longing to be clothed instead with your heavenly dwelling, because when you are clothed, you will not be found naked. For while you are in this tent, you groan and are burdened, because you do not wish to be unclothed but to be clothed instead with your heavenly dwelling, so that what is mortal may be swallowed up by life*. Now the One who has fashioned you for this very purpose is God, who has given you the Spirit as a deposit, guaranteeing what is to come.[2] In the resurrection of the dead your body is sown perishable, but raised imperishable. It is sown in dishonor; it is raised in glory. It is sown in weakness; it is raised in power. It is sown a natural body; it is raised a spiritual body. Just as you have borne the image of Adam, the man of dust, you shall also bear the image of Jesus Christ**, the man of heaven.[3] What you will be has not been made known. But you know that when Christ appears, you shall be like Him.[4]

Perfected mind and spirit: When the perfect comes, the partial will pass away.[5] For now you see in a mirror dimly, but then face to face.

---

[1] Rom 8:23 NIV
[2] 2Cor 5:1-5 NIV

[3] 1Cor 15:35,42-49 ESV

[4] 1John 3:2 NIV
[5] 1Cor 13:10 ESV

Now you know in part; then you shall know fully, even as you have been fully known by God.[6] Your spirit will be made perfect.[7]

...we know that when Christ appears, we shall be like Him, for we shall see Him as He is.

1 John 3:2 NIV

---

[6] 1Cor 13:12 ESV
[7] Heb 12:23 NASB

* Here the mortal bodies of believers on earth are com-pared to temporary tents. In heaven the "tent" is re-placed with a permanent dwell-ing—a redeemed, immortal body.

** *Literally*, the last Adam.

Your Imminent Departure

One of my favorite single-frame comics showed a man looking at the western sky from his porch, and superimposed on the sunset were the words THE END, like one might see at the end of a classic movie. He calls into the house, "Edith, come quick!" One day soon, whether through your death or through Christ's return to earth in glory, this comic will become your reality!

61. Physical Death: If You Should Die

> The phrase "If I should die before I wake" was a part of my bedtime prayer as a child. Early on I simply learned to recite these words, but eventually it hit me: wait, could that actually happen? Though you might not usually give it much thought, you would have to agree that today could actually be your last day on earth. A car accident, a heart attack, or any number of causes could suddenly bring your life on earth to a close. Since Christ was raised from the dead, however, you can be certain that you will likewise rise, and your death will prove to be your portal into Christ's presence. And after that, you can and will never die again!

Numbered days: God has determined your number of days.[1] All the days ordained for you were written in the Lord's book before one of them came to be.[2] Precious in the sight of the Lord is your death,[3] and you are blessed when you die in Him.[4] Should you find yourself away from the body you will be at home with the Lord.[5] On that very day you will be with Jesus in Paradise.[6]

Life triumphs: Your Savior Christ Jesus brought life to light for you through the gospel.[7] The Lord your God is from everlasting.[8] God so loved you that He gave His only Son,[9] that you will never[10] perish[11] but receive from Jesus[12] eternal life.[13] Your perishable body must put

---

[1] Job 14:5 NASB
[2] Ps 139:16 NIV
[3] Ps 116:15 NIV
[4] Rev 14:13 NIV
[5] 2Cor 5:8 NIV
[6] Luke 23:43 NKJV

[7] 2Tim 1:10 NKJV
[8] Hab 1:12 NKJV
[9] John 3:16 ESV
[10] John 10:28 NASB;
   cf. John 3:16

[11] John 3:16; 10:28
   NASB;
   cf. Hab 1:12
[12] John 10:28 NASB
[13] John 3:16; 10:28
   NASB

on the imperishable and your mortal body must put on immortality. When the perishable puts on the imperishable, and the mortal puts on immortality, then shall come to pass the saying that is written: "Death is swallowed up in victory." "O death, where is your victory? O death, where is your sting?" The sting of death is sin, and the power of sin is the law. But thanks be to God, who gives you the victory through your Lord Jesus Christ.[14] He has swallowed up death for you[15] forever[16] by His victory.[17]

Can't die again: At the resurrection you can no longer die; for you are like the angels. You are a child of the resurrection.[18] Though you die physically*, yet you shall live and never die.[19] You will not be hurt by the second death.[20]

Precious in the sight of the Lord is the death of His saints.

Psalm 116:15 ESV

---

[14] 1Cor 15:53-57 ESV
[15] Is 25:8; 1Cor 15:54 NKJV
[16] Is 25:8 NKJV

[17] 1Cor 15:54 NKJV
[18] Luke 20:33,36 NIV

[19] John 11:25-26 ESV; *cf.* Rev 21:4
[20] Rev 2:11 NASB

* *Literally,* die.

62. You Will See Christ Coming

Last year I packed up the family and set out to view a total solar eclipse. After weeks of preparation—ordering special glasses, finding the best viewing sites, and monitoring the weather—we were able to marvel at the darkened sun surrounded by its glowing corona. Birds went silent and the locusts began singing. It was an unforgettable spectacle! But there is another heavenly show that could occur at any moment, the likes of which has never before been seen. Christ will return in great power and glory and, for all those who have loved His appearing,[1] it will be a time of unimaginable joy! And all will see it with their own eyes—no special glasses required.

Christ is coming: You know that your Redeemer lives, and at the last Christ will stand upon the earth.[2] Jesus testified that He is the Christ, the Son of God,[3] and that one day you will see Him sitting at the right hand of the Mighty One[4] and coming on the clouds of heaven[5] with great power and glory.[6]

Gathering the elect: God will send out His angels[7] with a loud trumpet call,[8] and they will gather you along with all His elect from the four winds,[9] from the ends of the earth to the ends of the heavens.[10] Jesus Christ's winnowing fork will be in His hand, to clear His threshing floor and to gather you and all believers* into His barn**.[11] God will then receive you to glory.[12]

Raised with Christ: You will certainly be united with Jesus Christ in a resurrection like His.[13] God who raised the Lord Jesus will raise you also with Jesus.[14] Christ Himself will raise you up on the last day.[15]

---

[1] 2Tim 4:8 ESV
[2] Job 19:25 ESV
[3] Matt 26:63-64
   NASB;
   cf. Mark 14:61-62
[4] Matt 26:64 NIV;
   cf. Mark 14:62
[5] Matt 24:30 NKJV;
   cf. Matt 26:64;
   Mark 13:26; 14:62;

Luke 21:27
[6] Mark 13:26 NKJV;
   cf. Matt 24:30;
   Luke 21:27
[7] Matt 24:31 ESV;
   cf. Mark 13:27
[8] Matt 24:31 NIV
[9] Matt 24:31 NIV;
   cf. Mark 13:27

[10] Mark 13:27 NIV;
   cf. Matt 24:31
[11] Luke 3:17 NIV;
   cf. Matt 3:12
[12] Ps 73:24 ESV
[13] Rom 6:5 ESV;
   cf. Phil 3:10-11
[14] 2Cor 4:14 ESV
[15] John 6:40,39,54
   NASB

If you've already died: You believe that Jesus died[16] and has been raised from the dead,[17] the firstfruits[18] of those who have fallen asleep.[19] God will bring with Jesus those who have fallen asleep*** in Him.[20] The Lord Himself will descend from heaven and you, along with the rest of the dead in Christ, will rise first[21] and be made alive.[22] At the time of the end,[23] if you sleep in the dust of the earth,[24] with the sound of the trumpet of God[25] you shall awake[26] to everlasting life.[27] You shall live;[28] your body will be raised imperishable and immortal.[29]

If you're still alive: Otherwise you will be among those who are still alive, who are left until the coming of the Lord.[30] God revealed to you the things that must soon take place.[31] When these begin, you are encouraged to straighten up and lift up your head, because your redemption is drawing near.[32] You will be given strength to escape all these things and to stand before the Son of Man.[33] You will endure to the end and be saved.[34] The great tribulation[35] at the end of the age[36] will be shortened for your sake.[37] You will not precede those who have fallen asleep,[38] but you will be caught up together with them in the clouds to meet the Lord in the air.[39] Whether alive or asleep, you will be changed, in a moment, in the twinkling of an eye, at the last trumpet.[40]

"... you will see the Son of Man sitting at the right hand of the Mighty One and coming on the clouds of heaven."

Matthew 26:64 NIV

---

[16] 1Thes 4:14 NASB
[17] 1Cor 15:20 NASB; *cf.* 1Thes 4:14
[18] 1Cor 15:20,23 ESV
[19] 1Cor 15:20 ESV
[20] 1Thes 4:14 NIV
[21] 1Thes 4:16 NKJV
[22] 1Cor 15:22 NKJV
[23] Dan 11:40 NKJV
[24] Dan 12:2 NKJV; *cf.* Is 26:19
[25] 1Thes 4:16 ESV
[26] Dan 12:2 ESV; *cf.* Is 26:19
[27] Dan 12:2 NASB

[28] Is 26:19 ESV; *cf.* 1Cor 15:22
[29] 1Cor 15:54 ESV
[30] 1Thes 4:15 NIV
[31] Rev 1:1 NASB; *cf.* Mark 13:23; John 16:13; Rev 22:6
[32] Luke 21:28 NASB
[33] Luke 21:36 ESV
[34] Matt 24:13 NKJV
[35] Matt 24:21 NKJV; *cf.* Matt 24:29; Mark 13:24
[36] Matt 24:3 NKJV
[37] Matt 24:22 NKJV; *cf.* Mark 13:20

[38] 1Thes 4:15 NASB
[39] 1Thes 4:17 NASB
[40] 1Cor 15:51-52 NASB

* *Literally*, gather the wheat.

** Here Jesus compares the gathering of His elect on the day of His return to a farmer bringing in the harvest.

*** *Fallen asleep* is a euphemism for *died.*

Forever

Always with the Lord

Eternity is a really hard concept to wrap one's finite mind around. What will you be doing forever? Could you ever tire of it? Not in the least! Let's explore some of the promises about you being forever with the Lord.

63. You Live Forever

> Much of the Christian experience can be thought of as _already_, but _not yet_. Our experience of life in Christ now is a wonderful foretaste of the glorious life yet to come, but it is only a foretaste. The full extent of eternal life is yet to be experienced— and experience it you will! Everything mankind lost in the fall into sin will be more than fully restored when you enter life eternal. The tree of life in the Garden of Eden, once guarded by an angel with a fiery sword, will be fully accessible to you again. No more weeds, pain, sweat, or danger. And along with new heavens and a new earth, there will be a new you! You can only imagine!

Eternal life to come: Grace reigns for you.[1] Christ's righteous act has resulted in justification and life for you—you have been made righteous.[2] Therefore you are waiting for the mercy of your Lord Jesus Christ[3] in the age to come.[4] This mercy leads to[5] eternal life for you[6] through Jesus Christ your Lord.[7] You will live forever[8] because of Christ.[9] This is the promise that God made to you—eternal life.[10] Jesus Christ[11] will give to you the crown of life,[12] which God has promised to you.[13]

---

[1] Rom 5:21 NKJV
[2] Rom 5:18-19 NIV;
  _cf._ Rom 5:21
[3] Jude 1:21 ESV
[4] Luke 18:30 NASB
[5] Jude 1:21 ESV;
  _cf._ Rom 5:21; 6:22
[6] Jude 1:21 NASB;
  _cf._ Matt 25:46;

Luke 18:30; John
3:16; 6:40; Rom
5:21; 6:22; Gal 6:8
[7] Rom 5:21 NASB
[8] John 6:51,58
  NASB;
  _cf._ 1John 2:17
[9] John 6:57 NASB

[10] 1John 2:25 ESV;
  _cf._ 2Tim 1:1;
  Tit 1:2
[11] Rev 2:10 NASB
[12] Rev 2:10 NASB;
  _cf._ Jas 1:12
[13] Jas 1:12 ESV

Eden restored: You will have[14] the right to the tree of life,[15] which is in the Paradise of God, and you will eat of it.[16] The Lamb at the center of the throne will be your Shepherd, and He will lead you to springs of living water.[17] God will give you water without cost from the spring of the water of life.[18] The Lord will abolish the bow, the sword, and war, and He will make you lie down in safety.[19] You shall walk freely in heaven; no ravenous beast shall be found there.[20] In that day the Lord will make a covenant for you with the beasts of the field, the birds in the sky, and the creatures that move along the ground.[21] There the wolf and the lamb shall graze together; the lion shall eat straw like the ox, and dust shall be the serpent's food. They shall not hurt or destroy you.[22]

Immortality: Christ Jesus brought immortality to light for you through the gospel.[23] At the sound of last trumpet you will be raised imperishable and immortal.[24] You then experience the redemption of your body,[25] an eternal redemption secured through the blood of Christ.[26]

"... For My Father's will is that everyone who looks to the Son and believes in Him shall have eternal life...."

John 6:40 NIV

---

[14] Rev 22:14 NKJV
[15] Rev 22:14 NKJV;
  cf. Rev 2:7; 22:2
[16] Rev 2:7 NKJV
[17] Rev 7:17 NIV;
  cf. Rev 22:1
[18] Rev 21:6 NIV;
  cf. Rev 22:17
[19] Hos 2:18 ESV
[20] Is 35:9 NKJV
[21] Hos 2:18 NIV
[22] Is 65:25 ESV
[23] 2Tim 1:10 NASB
[24] 1Cor 15:52-53
  NASB
[25] Rom 8:23 NASB
[26] Heb 9:12 ESV

64. God's Wrath Is Fully Satisfied

In God's forever kingdom, His wrath against sin has been fully appeased. Sin has no hold over anyone there, and the fruit of the Spirit has full sway. Nothing remains to obscure God's amazing love, and nothing hinders you from seeing God face to face. Only those who by faith have received the salvation that Christ purchased for them are now present. Welcome to complete access and perfect acceptance!

No condemnation: Grace will be brought to you when Jesus Christ is revealed at His coming.[1] You will be saved[2] through the grace of your Lord Jesus Christ[3] from the wrath of God.[4] You do not come into judgment,[5] and you are not condemned[6]—you shall see the salvation of God.[7] For God has not destined you for wrath, but for obtaining salvation through your Lord Jesus Christ, who died for you, so that whether you are awake or asleep, you will live together with Him.[8] The Lord your God will save you on that day as a shepherd saves his flock.[9]

Enemies judged: God considers it just to repay with affliction those who afflict you, when the Lord Jesus is revealed from heaven with His mighty angels.[10]

[1] 1Pet 1:13 NIV
[2] Rom 5:9 ESV; cf. Matt 24:13; Mark 13:13; Acts 2:21; 15:11
[3] Acts 15:11 NIV; cf. Rom 5:9
[4] Rom 5:9 NASB
[5] John 5:24 NASB
[6] John 3:18 NKJV
[7] Luke 3:6 NASB
[8] 1Thes 5:9-10 NASB
[9] Zech 9:16 NIV
[10] 2Thes 1:6-7 ESV

...having now been justified by [Christ's] blood, we shall be saved from the wrath of God through Him.

Romans 5:9 NASB

65. You Are in His Presence Forever

Yes, you have already been adopted, but now you finally get to move into your new, permanent home. Talk about your desirable neighborhood! Picture your perfect home, including amenities, features, recreation, and stunning view. Can you picture it in your mind? Well, that's not even close to what it will be like. Scripture tells us no one can even imagine what God has prepared for those He loves—it will be that much better! And however wonderful heaven will be—and it will be wonderful for sure—it all pales in comparison to the ecstasy of being in the Lord's presence, face to face, soaking in the love that God Himself is.

Adoption finalized: In love God predestined you to adoption to Himself as His child through Jesus Christ.[1] You are a child of God.[2] You groan inwardly as you wait eagerly for your adoption as God's child.[3] God is your portion forever.[4]

Beyond reproach: Christ has now reconciled you in His fleshly body through death, in order to present you before Him holy and blameless and beyond reproach.[5] You are clothed[6] in fine[7] white[8] garments.[9] The Lord God has removed your disgrace from all the earth.[10]

Face to face: The Lord God brings you into His presence[11] forever.[12] Even after your skin has been destroyed, yet from your flesh you see God,[13] whom you see for yourself,[14] and your eyes see your Teacher.[15] You see God as He is,[16] face to face;[17] and your eyes behold the King in His beauty.[18] In the new heavens and new earth, before you call the Lord answers; while you are still speaking He hears.[19]

---

[1] Eph 1:4-5 NASB
[2] Luke 20:36 NASB
[3] Rom 8:23 ESV
[4] Ps 73:26 NASB
[5] Col 1:22 NASB
[6] Rev 3:5 NASB;
    cf. Zech 3:4
[7] Zech 3:4 NIV
[8] Rev 3:5 NKJV

[9] Rev 3:5 NKJV;
    Zech 3:4 NIV
[10] Is 25:8 ESV;
    cf. Jude 1:24
[11] 2Cor 4:14 ESV;
    cf. Ps 41:12
[12] Ps 41:12 NASB
[13] Job 19:26 NASB
[14] Job 19:27 ESV

[15] Is 30:20 ESV;
    cf. Rev 1:7
[16] 1John 3:2 NIV; cf.
    Is 30:20; Matt 5:8;
    1Cor 13:12
[17] 1Cor 13:12 NIV;
    cf. Ps 11:7;
    Rev 22:4
[18] Is 33:17 ESV
[19] Is 65:17,24 NIV

With the Lord: When Christ who is your life appears, then you also appear with Him in glory.[20] At the coming of the Lord,[21] you are always with Him[22] and live with Him.[23] God dwells with you, and you are one of His people, and God Himself is with you as your God.[24] You are before the throne of God, and serve Him day and night in His temple.[25] Jesus the Messiah, the Son of[26] David, is your Prince forever.[27] The Lord has set His sanctuary in your midst forevermore.[28]

The Joy of Jesus: In the new heavens and new earth, the Lord rejoices and is glad in you.[29] Jesus declared to you, "Well done, good and faithful servant. You have been faithful over a little; I am setting you over much." You have entered into the joy of your Master**.[30]

... You set me in Your presence forever.
Psalm 41:12 NASB

---

[20] Col 3:4 ESV
[21] 1Thes 4:15 NASB
[22] 1Thes 4:17 ESV; cf. Luke 23:43; Rev 17:14
[23] 2Tim 2:11 NASB
[24] Rev 21:3 ESV; cf. Ezek 37:27; Zech 8:8
[25] Rev 7:15 NKJV
[26] Matt 1:1 NASB

[27] Ezek 37:25 NASB
[28] Ezek 37:26 NKJV
[29] Is 65:17,19 NASB
[30] Matt 25:21,23 ESV

* Sinful man cannot look on God's face and live (Ex 33:20), but having received the right-eousness of Christ, this barrier has been eliminated.

** Here believers at Christ's return are compared to faithful stewards at their master's return.

66. You Enter the Kingdom of Heaven

You are on the honored guest list, and the door of God's king-dom swings wide open. Jesus has completed your room with all the special touches He knows will communicate to you how very much He loves you. There you are welcomed by your amazing God—Father, Son, and Holy Spirit. And if that weren't enough, you get to enjoy talking with saints throughout the ages, including Noah, Abraham, Ruth, David, Isaiah, Es-ther, Mary, the Gospel writers, the Apostle Paul, and the list goes on and on. And they will be just as excited to meet you and learn your story! You don't have to fumble for a ticket or find a phone app—you are recognized immediately and lov-ingly ushered in.

Authorized entry: Entrance into the eternal kingdom of our Lord and Savior Jesus Christ has been richly provided for you.[1] The Lord brings you to dwell in the midst of[2] the holy city, New[3] Jerusalem.[4] You enter the city by the gates.[5]

A place prepared: God has prepared a city for you.[6] Behold, the dwell-ing place of God is with you.[7] The Lord appoints a place for you as one of His people. He plants you that you may dwell in your own place and be disturbed no more.[8] The Lord is your God and you are His child.[9] You will dwell in the house of the Lord forever.[10] Jesus' Father's house has many rooms; if that were not so, would Jesus have told you that He went to prepare a place for you? Since He did go and prepare a place for you, Jesus will come back[11] and take you to be with Him that you also will be where He is.[12]

Celebrating together: Blessed are you, who have received an invita-tion* to the wedding supper of the Lamb[13]—a white stone** with a new name written on it.[14] You eat and drink at Christ's table in His kingdom.[15] Christ drinks of the fruit of the vine new with you here.[16]

[1] 2Pet 1:11 ESV
[2] Zech 8:8 ESV
[3] Rev 21:2 NKJV
[4] Zech 8:8;
   Rev 21:2 ESV
[5] Rev 22:14 ESV
[6] Heb 11:16 NKJV
[7] Rev 21:3 ESV;
   cf. Ezek 37:27
[8] 1Chron 17:9 ESV
[9] Rev 21:7 NKJV
[10] Ps 23:6 NIV
[11] John 14:2-3 NIV
[12] John 14:3 NIV;
   cf. 2Tim 2:11
[13] Rev 19:9 NIV
[14] Rev 2:17 NIV
[15] Luke 22:30 NIV
[16] Mark 14:25; Matt
   26:29 NASB

You take your place at the feast in the kingdom of God[17] with many[18] people[19] from east and west[20] and north and south,[21] including Abraham, Isaac, and Jacob.[22] The Lord changed your speech and that of all believers*** to a pure speech, that all of you may call upon the name of the Lord and serve Him with one accord.[23] The throne of God and of the Lamb are in the city, and you and all His servants now worship Him there.[24]

...there will be richly provided for you an entrance into the eternal kingdom of our Lord and Savior Jesus Christ.

2 Peter 1:11 ESV

---

[17] Luke 13:29 NIV;
   cf. Matt 8:11
[18] Matt 8:11 NASB
[19] Luke 13:29 ESV
[20] Luke 13:29
   NASB;
   cf. Matt 8:11
[21] Luke 13:29 NIV

[22] Matt 8:11 NIV
[23] Zeph 3:9 ESV
[24] Rev 22:3 ESV

* *Literally,* are invited.

** See *white stone* in glossary.

*** *Literally,* the peoples.

Forever

All Things Made New[1]

No human mind has ever come close to knowing what is in store for God's beloved. But here are some great previews of the changes to come.

67. The Former Things Have Passed Away

Pain, disappointment, broken promises, injuries, hurt feelings, and exhaustion—all these have been such a consistent part of your life here in this fallen world that they may almost seem normal. But they are not—they never were a part of God's intent for you. Not only can *you* be frustrated and discouraged by such events, but creation itself is "groaning," eager for the restoration to Eden's perfection and beyond. In heaven, all such "former things" are gone for good. From day-one in God's kingdom and forever after that, your new life will be joyful, safe, secure, exciting, creative, and satisfying in ways beyond what you can now comprehend.

No more crying or mourning: In the new heavens and new earth,[2] the sound of weeping and of crying is heard no more.[3] Your Lord Jesus Christ Himself and God your Father will comfort your heart.[4] Your days of[5] crying[6] and mourning will have ended,[7] for such former things have passed away.[8] God will wipe away every tear from your eyes.[9] The Lord will turn your mourning to[10] everlasting[11] joy[12] and laughter;[13] He will comfort you,[14] and give you gladness for sorrow.[15] The Lord has spoken this to you.[16]

No more sickness or pain: God grants relief to you who are afflicted.[17] In heaven, you will never say, "I am sick."[18] You won't experience

---

[1] Rev 21:5 NASB
[2] Is 65:17 NASB
[3] Is 65:19 NIV
[4] 2Thes 2:16-17 NASB
[5] Is 60:20 NIV
[6] Rev 21:4 NIV
[7] Is 60:20 ESV; cf. Rev 21:4
[8] Rev 21:4 NKJV
[9] Rev 21:4 NKJV; cf. Is 25:8; Rev 7:17
[10] Jer 31:13 NKJV; cf. Matt 5:4
[11] Is 35:10 NKJV
[12] Jer 31:13; Is 35:10 NKJV
[13] Luke 6:21 NKJV
[14] Jer 31:13 NKJV; cf. Matt 5:4
[15] Jer 31:13 ESV; cf. Is 35:10
[16] Is 25:8 NASB
[17] 2Thes 1:7 ESV
[18] Is 33:24 NKJV

pain any more, for the former things have passed away.[19] You go out leaping like a calf from the stall.[20]

Every need met: At the Lord's right hand are pleasures forevermore.[21] You rest from your labors.[22] You hunger no longer, nor thirst anymore.[23] The sun does not beat down on you, nor any scorching heat.[24]

Completely secure: You dwell securely.[25] The Lord has made an everlasting covenant of peace with you.[26] The New[27] Jerusalem[28] is holy, and strangers shall never again pass through it.[29] Nothing impure[30] or accursed[31] ever enters it, nor anyone who does what is shameful or deceitful, but only you and all those whose names are written in the Lamb's book of life.[32] Wicked people will not oppress you anymore.[33]

Everlasting salvation: You are saved by the Lord with everlasting salvation;[34] you will not be put to shame or humiliated to all eternity.[35]

"[God] will wipe away every tear from their eyes, and death shall be no more, neither shall there be mourning, nor crying, nor pain anymore, for the former things have passed away."

Revelation 21:4 ESV

---

[19] Rev 21:4 NKJV
[20] Mal 4:2 ESV
[21] Ps 16:11 NKJV
[22] Rev 14:13 NASB
[23] Rev 7:16 NASB
[24] Rev 7:16 NIV
[25] Jer 23:6 NASB
[26] Ezek 37:26 NASB
[27] Rev 21:2 NKJV
[28] Rev 21:2 NKJV;
  cf. Joel 3:17
[29] Joel 3:17 ESV
[30] Rev 21:27 NIV
[31] Rev 22:3 ESV
[32] Rev 21:27 NIV;
  cf. Rev 22:3
[33] 1Chron 17:9 NIV
[34] Is 45:17 ESV;
  cf. Heb 5:9
[35] Is 45:17 NASB

68. You Receive Your Full Inheritance

When you think of receiving an inheritance, perhaps old movies may come to mind about a room full of relatives waiting to hear the reading of their rich uncle's will and to find out what portion of the estate may be passing to them. Since God has already provided you such rich blessings, your first thought may be, "There's more?" Apparently, there is—riches beyond telling! But you may not be so sure that this is meant for you—perhaps for great men of faith like Abraham or Paul, but certainly God couldn't mean you! But as God's inheritance is distributed, there is no question that your name has been plainly called. You are awe-struck!

Inheritance assigned: The Father has qualified you to share in the inheritance of the saints in light,[1] and your inheritance endures forever.[2] You will have obtained[3] the promised eternal[4] inheritance[5] from the Lord[6] as your reward.[7] You will be experiencing the riches of God's glorious inheritance in you.[8]

Inheritance realized: You are blessed[9] by Christ's Father[10] and will have taken your inheritance,[11] the kingdom[12] prepared for you since the creation of the world.[13] Christ has assigned this kingdom to you,[14] and it is your Father's good pleasure to give it to you.[15] When the Ancient of Days has come,[16] you with all the saints of the Most High receive the kingdom.[17] You possess[18] and dwell in[19] the kingdom[20] forever—yes, forever and ever.[21] The kingdom you receive cannot be shaken.[22]

[1] Col 1:12 ESV
[2] Ps 37:18 NIV
[3] Eph 1:11 NASB; cf. Col 3:24; Heb 9:15
[4] Heb 9:15 NIV
[5] Heb 9:15 NIV; cf. Eph 1:11; Col 3:24;
[6] Col 3:24 NIV; cf. Eph 1:11
[7] Col 3:24 ESV
[8] Eph 1:18 NIV
[9] Matt 25:34 NIV; cf. Matt 5:3,5,10; Luke 6:20
[10] Matt 25:34 NIV
[11] Matt 25:34 NIV; cf. Is 57:13; Matt 5:5
[12] Matt 25:34 NIV; cf. Matt 5:3,10; Luke 6:20
[13] Matt 25:34 NIV
[14] Luke 22:29 ESV
[15] Luke 12:32 NKJV
[16] Dan 7:22 NKJV
[17] Dan 7:18 NKJV; cf. Gen 17:8
[18] Dan 7:18,22 NKJV; cf. Gen 17:8
[19] Ps 37:29 NKJV
[20] Dan 7:18,22 NKJV
[21] Dan 7:18 NIV; cf. Gen 17:8
[22] Heb 12:28 NASB

Righteousness: The Lord has laid up for you the crown of righteous-ness, awarded to you on the day[23] of Christ's appearing.[24] For you the sun of righteousness has risen with healing in its rays.[25] Since the Lord is your righteousness,[26] you are righteous.[27] Your hunger and thirst for righteousness are satisfied.[28] You are one of the Lord's people, and He is your God, in truth and righteousness.[29]

In [Christ] we have obtained an inheritance, having been predestined according to the purpose of Him who works all things according to the counsel of His will.

Ephesians 1:11 ESV

---

[23] 2Tim 4:8 NASB

[24] 2Tim 4:1 NIV

[25] Mal 4:2 NIV

[26] Jer 23:6 NASB

[27] Is 60:21 NASB

[28] Matt 5:6 NASB

[29] Zech 8:8 NASB

69. The Glory of the Lord Is Revealed

> You are going to shine in glory forever. Yes, you! And all who have ever believed will marvel at what God has done in and through you. You are to reign with your Lord Jesus Christ forever! The day of your complete salvation is indeed closer now than it was on the day you first believed. It could be today!

Unimaginable glory: What no eye has seen, nor ear heard, nor the heart of man imagined, God has prepared for you—these things He has revealed to you through the Spirit.[1] God called you through the Gospel to share in the glory of our Lord Jesus Christ,[2] and God is bringing you to glory.[3] You are a partaker of[4] the glory that is going to be revealed,[5] and all people will see it together with you.[6] You shall shine[7] forever and ever[8] like a jewel of a crown,[9] like the stars, like the brightness of the sky above,[10] and like the sun[11] in the kingdom of your Father.[12]

Everlasting light: When the chief Shepherd appears, you receive the unfading crown of glory.[13] The Lord of hosts will be a crown of glory and a diadem of beauty to you.[14] You will need no light[15] of lamp[16] or sun,[17] for the Lord God will be[18] your everlasting[19] light[20] and your glory.[21]

Glorified in you: The Lord Jesus comes on that day[22] when He is revealed,[23] to be glorified in you[24] and to be marveled at among all who have believed.[25]

[1] 1Cor 2:9-10 ESV
[2] 2Thes 2:14 NIV
[3] Heb 2:10 NASB
[4] 1Pet 5:1 NASB
[5] Is 40:5 ESV; cf. Rom 8:18; 1Pet 5:1
[6] Is 40:5 NIV
[7] Matt 13:43 NKJV; cf. Dan 12:3, Zech 9:16
[8] Dan 12:3 NKJV
[9] Zech 9:16 ESV
[10] Dan 12:3 ESV
[11] Matt 13:43 NIV
[12] Matt 13:43 NIV; cf. 1Chron 29:11
[13] 1Pet 5:4 NASB
[14] Is 28:5 ESV
[15] Rev 22:5 ESV; cf. Is 60:19-20; Rev 21:23
[16] Rev 22:5 ESV; cf. Rev 21:23
[17] Rev 22:5 ESV; cf. Is 60:19-20; Rev 21:23
[18] Rev 22:5 ESV; cf. Is 60:19-20
[19] Is 60:19-20 NIV
[20] Is 60:19-20 NIV; cf. Rev 21:23; 22:5
[21] Is 60:19 NIV
[22] 2Thes 1:10 ESV
[23] 2Thes 1:7 NKJV; cf. Is 44:23 NIV
[24] 2Thes 1:10; Is 44:23 NKJV
[25] 2Thes 1:10 NASB

Reigning forever: Your reward is great[26] in heaven.[27] You will reign[28] forever and ever[29] with Christ Jesus,[30] and God will exalt you.[31] Jesus Christ will grant you to sit with Him on His throne, as He also sat down with His Father on His throne.[32]

Then the glory of the Lord will be revealed. And all flesh will see it together; For the mouth of the Lord has spoken.

Isaiah 40:5 NASB

---

[26] Luke 6:23 NASB;
  cf. Luke 6:35
[27] Luke 6:23 NASB

[28] Rev 5:10 NASB;
  cf. 2Tim 2:12;
  Rev 22:5
[29] Rev 22:5 NKJV

[30] 2Tim 2:12 NKJV
[31] Jas 4:10 NASB;
  cf. 1Pet 5:6
[32] Rev 3:21 NKJV

That You May Know

YOUR TRIP SUMMARY

70. The Coming Ages

> Jesus Christ is indeed the same yesterday, today, and forever. You did not choose God, but He chose you. Before creation God established His plan to love you and save you from your sins. He brought you to Himself, He created faith in your heart, and He has given you new life and has exalted you. My prayer is that, throughout your life, you will continue to explore and savor all that God in Christ has done for you, continues to do today, and promises to do throughout all eternity. God is faithful, and He will bring it to pass. And in Christ, all of His promises to you are most assuredly YES!

Because of His great love for you, God, who is rich in mercy, made you alive with Christ even when you were dead in transgressions—it is by grace you have been saved. And God raised you up with Christ and seated you with Him in the heavenly realms in Christ Jesus, in order that in the coming ages He might show the incomparable riches of His grace, expressed in His kindness to you in Christ Jesus.[1]

Together with the Holy Spirit and all other believers, you say to your Lord Jesus, "Come."[2] He replies to you, "Yes, I am coming soon."[3] Amen. Come Lord Jesus![4]

He who testifies to these things says, "Surely I am coming soon." Amen. Come Lord Jesus!
Revelation 22:20 ESV

---

[1] Eph 2:4-7 NIV
[2] Rev 22:17 NIV
[3] Rev 22:20 NIV
[4] Rev 22:20 ESV

That You May Know

Bible Book Abbreviations

Book of Bible	Abbr.
Acts	Acts
Amos	Amos
Chronicles, 1st	1Chron
Chronicles, 2nd	2Chron
Colossians	Col
Corinthians, 1st	1Cor
Corinthians, 2nd	2Cor
Daniel	Dan
Deuteronomy	Deut
Ecclesiastes	Eccl
Ephesians	Eph
Exodus	Ex
Ezekiel	Ezek
Ezra	Ezra
Galatians	Gal
Genesis	Gen
Habakkuk	Hab
Haggai	Hag
Hebrews	Heb
Hosea	Hos
Isaiah	Is
James	Jas
Jeremiah	Jer
Job	Job
Joel	Joel
John	John
John, 1st	1John
John, 2nd	2John
Jonah	Jonah

Joshua	Josh
Jude	Jude
Kings, 1st	1King
Kings, 2nd	2King
Lamentations	Lam
Leviticus	Lev
Luke	Luke
Malachi	Mal
Mark	Mark
Matthew	Matt
Micah	Micah
Nehemiah	Neh
Numbers	Num
Peter, 1st	1Pet
Peter, 2nd	2Pet
Philemon	Phm
Philippians	Phil
Proverbs	Prov
Psalms	Ps
Revelation	Rev
Romans	Rom
Samuel, 1st	1Sam
Samuel, 2nd	2Sam
Thessalonians, 1st	1Thes
Thessalonians, 2nd	2Thes
Timothy, 1st	1Tim
Timothy, 2nd	2Tim
Titus	Tit
Zechariah	Zech
Zephaniah	Zeph

Glossary

Abba
Endearing Aramaic term for father or daddy; one of an infant's first words like "dada"; surprisingly familiar word with which to address our heavenly Father!

anointed
Shepherds poured oil upon (anointed) their sheep's heads, causing dangerous insects to slide off and preventing them from entering the sheep's ears and nose and causing the sheep harm or death. For people, being anointed indicates receiving a blessing, protection, empowerment, or a formal calling to a spiritual leadership role.[1]

antichrist
Opposite to Christ; someone acting in place of (against) Christ.[2]

atoned
Literally means covered. *Covered* sins is used as an idiom for *forgiven* sins.[3]

blessed
In an enviable position from having received God's provision or favor.[4]

body (of Christ)
The collection of believers in Christ, whose Head is Christ.

buckler
Small, round shield for one's left arm, held by a handle at arm's length.[5]

church
Literally, an assembly of people. A local group of believers that worship and study together, or the entire collection of believers on earth.

crucified
Shameful and excruciatingly painful execution by suffocation, with arms bound to a suspended beam of wood (cross).

curtain
A massively thick curtain or veil restricted entry into the Most Holy Place of the Jewish temple to all except the high priest once a year. Through Christ's once-for-all sacrifice of Himself, all believers enjoy unrestricted access to God, symbolically "through the curtain."

delivered	Removed from the midst of danger or oppression; drawn to God Himself, rescued or snatched out.[6]
disciple	A student or apprentice; a follower of Jesus Christ, including the original twelve chosen and appointed by Him, along with all who believe in Him because of their word.
dominion	The position of headship and stewardship that human beings have over creation.[7]
elect	Chosen one; one who is chosen by God.
evil	Absence of goodness, morally wrong, sinful, wicked; anything that causes harm.[8] The *evil one* refers to the devil.[9]
forgiven	Released or pardoned from one's debt of sins before God.
fortress	Stronghold, castle; anything upon which one relies.[10]
fruit	Metaphor for everything done in true partnership with Christ; includes good works.[11]
glorified	Made glorious, adorned with luster or light, clothed with splendor; praised, extolled, magnified, celebrated.[12]
horn	Symbol of strength, power, potency, or victory.[13]
iniquities	*See* **sins**.
intercession	Literally, assailing with petitions; the process of pleading or urging on someone's behalf.[14]
justified	Rendered or declared righteous before God for Christ's sake.
manna, hidden	In Rev 2:17, likely an allusion to receiving Christ Himself. A portion of the heavenly bread (manna) provided to the Israelites by God in the wilderness was hidden away in the Ark of the Covenant, which the Jews believed would be found again in the end times. Jesus declared Himself to be the Bread of Life, that came down from heaven (John 6:48-51).[15] In the Passover

celebration, the second of three pieces of unleavened bread is broken and hidden away in a cloth pouch, to be brought out again later. This marvelous picture of Christ's suffering, death, burial and resurrection was perhaps the very bread that Christ broke and shared with His disciples at the Lord's Supper on the night in which He was betrayed.[16]

reconciled   Brought into a state of favor with God.[17]

redemption   The price God paid to buy you back (redeem you) from your sins.

regeneration   Being born again; restitution of all things.[18]

restoration   Returning something to original condition; in Christ, receiving back more than what was lost.[19]

righteousness   State of being faultless and guiltless before God —only possible as God's gift.

saint   A holy one, separated from the world and consecrated to God; a believer in Christ.

sanctification   The process of making or becoming holy, set apart, or consecrated.

saved   Healed, preserved, rescued, or delivered out of danger to safety.[20]

shepherd   Keeper of sheep; used to describe a king's benevolent leadership of his subjects.

sins   Instances of "missing the mark"—breaking God's law. Sin is expressed by several terms in the Bible. *Trespasses* involve "crossing the line" to outside God's will, whether intentional or not. *Transgressions* are deliberate, premeditated trespasses.[21] *Iniquities* are more about moving the mark or changing the lines. This involves redefining God's law to one's self-justification.[22]

soul   A person, a person's life; the seat of feelings, desires, affections, and aversions. Persists after physical death, at times used synonymously with *spirit*.[23]

spirit	That which animates a body and gives it life; the power to think, feel, and decide. Often used in parallel with the term *heart*. Persists after physical death, at times used synonymously with *soul*.[24]
sprinkled	Ceremonial cleansing and purification performed in Old Testament sacrifices, applied in the New Testament to the sinner made clean through the shed blood of Christ.[25]
steadfast love	God's persistent, unconditional tenderness, kindness, and mercy; a relationship in which God seeks after man with love and mercy.[26]
transgressions	*See* **sins**.
trespasses	*See* **sins**.
white stone	In New Testament times, it was a tradition for people hosting a victory banquet to provide special white stones for invitees to gain admission. Rev 2:17 probably entails receiving one's personalized invitation to the Lord's heavenly banquet. The new name in this verse likely highlights one's intimate relationship with the Lord Jesus Christ.[27]
wrath (of God)	God's anger and passion in opposition to sin; punishment and vengeance for unforgiven sin.[28]

[1] What is the anointing? ©2002-2019 Got Questions Ministry, www.gotquestions.org/anointed.html; A Shepherd Looks at Psalm 23, Phillip Keller, © 1970, Zondervan, pp. 111ff.
[2] 500. antichristos, Strong's Concordance, ©2004-2018 by Bible Hub, biblehub.com/greek/500.htm
[3] Hebrew Lexicon entry for Kaphar, The NAS Old Testament Hebrew Lexicon, Brown, Driver, Briggs and Gesenius, www.biblestudytools.com/lexicons/hebrew/nas/kaphar.html
[4] 3107. makarios, Strong's Concordance, ©2004-2018 by Bible Hub, biblehub.com/greek/3107.htm
[5] Buckler, Merriam-Webster Dictionary: www.merriam-webster.com/dictionary/buckler

[6] 4506. rhuomai, Strong's Concordance, ©1992-2019 Church of the Great God, biblehub.com/greek/4506.htm

[7] Called to Believe, Teach, and Confess: An Introduction to Doctrinal Theology, edited by Stephen P. Mueller, ©2005, Wipf & Stock Publishers, Eugene, OR, p. 514.

[8] What is the definition of evil? ©2002-2019 Got Questions Ministries, last updated: Feb. 14, 2019, https://www.gotquestions.org/definition-of-evil.html

[9] Nelson's Compact Bible Dictionary, Ronald F. Youngblood, E.F. Bruce & R.K. Harrison, ©2004 Thomas Nelson Publishers, "Devil" p. 181.

[10] Ochuroma, Thayer's Greek Lexicon, ©1992-2019 Church of the Great God, www.bibletools.org/index.cfm/fuseaction/Lexicon.show/ID/G3794/ochuroma.htm

[11] 2590. karpos, HELPS Word-studies ©1987, 2011, Thayer's Greek Lexicon ©2002, 2003, 2006, 2011 by Biblesoft, Inc., ©2004-2018 by Bible Hub, biblehub.com/greek/2590.htm

[12] Doxazo, Thayer's Greek Lexicon, ©1992-2019 Church of the Great God, www.bibletools.org/index.cfm/fuseaction/Lexicon.show/ID/G1392/doxazo.htm

[13] What is the horn of salvation? ©2002-2019 Got Questions Ministries, last updated: Feb. 14, 2019, https://www.gotquestions.org/horn-of-salvation.html

[14] Intercession, Baker's Evangelical Dictionary of Biblical Theology, ©1996 Walter A. Elwell, https://www.biblestudytools.com/dictionary/intercession/

[15] The International Standard Bible Encyclopedia, Volume Three: K-P, Geoffrey W. Bromiley, ed., ©1986 Wm. B. Eerdmans Publishing Company, Grand Rapids, MI, "Manna," pp. 239-240.

[16] A Passover Haggadah for Christians, Bruce J. Lieske, ed. 1985, pp. 11, 23-24.

[17] Reconciliation, KJV Dictionary Definition ©2019 AV1611.com, av1611.com/kjbp/kjv-dictionary/reconciliation.html

[18] Regeneration, Baker's Evangelical Dictionary of Biblical Theology, ©1996 Walter A. Elwell, www.biblestudytools.com/dictionary/regeneration/

[19] Coming to Terms: Restoration, Steve Johnson, Insight for Living Canada, Dec. 7, 2018, www.insightforliving.ca/read.articles/coming-terms-restoration

[20] Sozo, Thayer's Greek Lexicon, ©1992-2019 Church of the Great God, www.bibletools.org/index.cfm/fuseaction/Lexicon.show/ID/G4982/sozo.htm

[21] Sins, Trespasses, Trangression & Iniquities have different meanings, Notes from Perry Stone's study, Sep. 23, 2012, https://runningtowardsinfinity.blogspot.com/2012/09/sins-trespasses-transgression.html?m=1

[22] What Are Iniquities and How Are They Different Than Our Sins?, Mike Leake, ©2019, Crosswalk.com, https://www.crosswalk.com/faith/bible-study/what-are-iniquities-and-how-are-they-different-than-our-sins.html

[23] Psuche, The KJV New Testament Greek Lexicon, ©2019, Bible Study Tools, https://www.biblestudytools.com/lexicons/greek/kjv/psuche.html

[24] Pneuma, The NAS New Testament Greek Lexicon, ©2019, Bible Study Tools, https://www.biblestudytools.com/lexicons/greek/nas/pneuma.html

[25] Sprinkle; Sprinkling, International Standard Bible Encyclopedia, Orr, James, M.A., D.D. General Editor, 1915, www.biblestudytools.com/dictionary/sprinkle-sprinkling/

[26] Lovingkindness-Definition of Kesed, Precept Austin, Updated Mar. 5, 2018, https://www.preceptaustin.org/lovingkindness-definition_of_hesed

[27] Why is God going to give us a white stone with a new name? ©2002-2019 Got Questions Ministries, https://www.gotquestions.org/white-stone-new-name.html

[28] 3709. orge, Strong's Concordance; HELPS Word-studies ©1987, 2011 by Helps Ministries, Inc.; Thayer's Greek Lexicon, ©2002, 2003, 2006, 2011 by BibleSoft.com; https://biblehub.com/greek/3709.htm